HEBREW INSIGHTS FROM REVELATION

Eli Lizorkin-Eyzenberg
& Pinchas Shir

JEWISH STUDIES
FOR CHRISTIANS

ISBN: 9798764519982

Table of Contents

Introduction 4

Chapter 1: Revelation as a Jewish Apocalypse 6

Chapter 2: The Hebrew Structure of Revelation 18

Chapter 3: Revelation as a Letter to Real People 26

Chapter 4: The Lord's Day 43

Chapter 5: Letters within a Letter 65

Chapter 6: God's Throne 127

Chapter 7: The Seven Seals 157

In Closing 177

Bibliography 179

Introduction

The book of Revelation is a first-century Jewish document that recognizes Jesus as Emperor of worldwide Emprire. Most people find it hard to understand. It speaks of heavenly visions and refers to prophecies many have tried to unlock and understand - with many different interpretations.

For many centuries, this book's interpretation has been almost solely in the hands of those unfamiliar with Jewish language or culture. Therefore, the cultural and linguistic disconnect was substantial.

When we decided to write a book on Revelation, we knew we could not endeavor to write a comprehensive verse-by-verse commentary on the entire book. Maybe someday we will devote sufficient effort to such an aspiration. However, unfazed by our inability to cover the entire book, we felt that we could at least establish a new trajectory for re-reading Revelation. We desire to show how this book can be read and present some overlooked (but important) caveats. That is what this book is about.

We begin by taking the first six chapters and slowly walking you through our reading of those chapters. We try to move systematically verse by verse—establishing a clear method of reading Revelation in a way it is rarely read today.

Rather than be comprehensive and provide detailed academic footnotes for our research, we decided to write the book in an uncluttered style accessible to everyone. Most of the works we reference are other ancient books (original sources), some Greco-Roman and historical writings, and occasional sources on Christian tradition. We also mention several modern works on the topic (secondary sources). We are indebted to these for many details we have chosen to highlight.

Come with us on a journey of discovery and reread the Book of Revelation in a way that it was not read by you before.

Pinchas Shir &
Eli Lizorkin-Eyezenberg

Chapter 1: Revelation as a Jewish Apocalypse

Some Christians may find it surprising that the book of the Bible most people know as "The Revelation of St. John" is actually a thoroughly Jewish book. To us, it is obvious from the very first lines of the text. The author opens his message in a fashion strikingly similar to other Jewish apocalyptic texts but that assumes familiarity with other Jewish books of similar genre. For now, look carefully at the opening:

> ***The revelation of Jesus Christ, which God gave Him to show to His bond-servants, the things which must soon take place; and He sent and communicated it by His angel to His bond-servant John, who testified to the word of God and to the testimony of Jesus Christ, even to all that he saw (Rev. 1:1-2).***[1]

The author explains what he writes (revelation of Jesus Christ) and why it was given (to show to his bond-servants the things which must soon take place). The opening tells us how it was given (God sent and communicated it by His angel) and who, in fact, was the primary recipient of this revelation (his bond-servant, John, who testified to all that he saw; to the word of God and to the testimony of Jesus Christ). In some

---

[1] Unless otherwise noted the text of Revelation is quoted from New American Standard Bible with minor adaptations by the authors.

ways, Revelation resembles other apocalyptic Jewish books, and in other ways, it stands completely apart.

By the way, "Jesus Christ" is a fundamentally Jewish name and a title. Jesus is Yeshua (ישוע, *yeshua*) a first century shortened version of the name Joshua or Yehoshua (יהושע). That is Jesus' actual name, a name by which he was known to his parents, friends, and to his followers. It comes from the Hebrew verb "to save" (להושיע, *lehoshiah*). Christ is a Jewish idea of someone "anointed" or literally "smeared in oil" – Mashiach (משיח) a leader who was called and set apart for a special mission. This term would not make much sense in the greater Hellenistic culture, but Jews receiving this text would recall that prophets, priests, and kings were ceremonially anointed for the task of leading God's people. And that is what this term communicates.

Revelation combines apocalyptic, epistolary, and prophetic styles of Jewish literature. It is simultaneously a heavenly vision about the end of days, a letter, and a prophecy. But looking at other Jewish apocalyptic books, we can recognize that such an opening is not just typical but entirely predictable for this Jewish literary genre. Let us briefly look at how another well-known apocalyptic Jewish book opens:

> The word of the blessing of Enoch, how he blessed the elect and the righteous, who were to exist in the time of trouble, rejecting all the wicked and ungodly. Enoch, a righteous man, who was with God, answered and spoke while his eyes were open and while he saw a holy vision in the heavens. This the angels showed me. From them, I heard all things and

> understood what I saw; that which will not take
> place in this generation but in a generation
> which is to succeed at a distant period, on
> account of the elect. (1 Enoch 1:1-2)

Do you notice the similarity? Let's look into another
Jewish book, entitled the Apocalypse of Baruch, which
begins in a similar manner:

> Verily I Baruch was weeping in my mind and
> sorrowing on account of the people, and that
> Nebuchadnezzar the king was permitted by
> God to destroy His city …and behold as I was
> weeping and saying such things, I saw an angel
> of the Lord coming and saying to me:
> Understand, O man, greatly beloved, and
> trouble not thyself so greatly concerning the
> salvation of Jerusalem, for thus saith the Lord
> God, the Almighty. For He sent me before
> thee, to make known and to show to thee all
> (the things) …and the angel of the powers said
> to me, Come, and I will show thee the
> mysteries of God. (3 Baruch 1:1-8 /Apocalypse
> of Baruch)

These quoted passages demonstrate plainly that what
we read in Revelation's opening verses is, in fact,
strikingly similar to other Jewish apocalyptic accounts
from around the same time period. Why? Did John
plagiarize? Of course not. But he was writing an
apocalypse, and with that comes conventions of a genre
familiar to his contemporaries. His book needed to
signal that it is similar to other books from this genre,
so he simply followed the expected formula. That's why
these openings all sound alike.

In Greek, the word for "revelation" is ἀποκάλυψις *(apokalupsis)*. The scary English word "apocalypse" comes from this Greek word. Contrary to its negative connotations, this word has nothing to do with ominous catastrophes or disasters of any sort. It carries no connotations of doom or the end of the world. It simply means "to reveal something that was hidden".

The oldest manuscripts of "John's Revelation" we have today are in Greek. John was unquestionably a multi-lingual Jew, as were many of his contemporaries. But it is still hard to imagine Jesus speaking to John in Greek (his non-native language) in heaven. Though the text we possess today is in Greek, imagining the Hebrew subtext gives us a great interpretive advantage. We can stand closer to the actual events that occurred in John's series of visions if we explore them in the context of ancient Hebrew.

Take the Hebrew word for "revelation" for example. It is הִתְגַּלּוּת *(hitgalut),* and its basic meaning is not much different from its Greek counterpart. It simply means to "uncover something that was hidden" The term comes from verb גָּלָה *(galah),* which means "to uncover", "to disclose" and "to expose". It is a common verb used hundreds of times in the Hebrew Bible. There is another common Hebrew word that sounds a lot like הִתְגַּלּוּת *(hitgalut)* - גָּלוּת *(galut).* It means "exile" and describes what happened to Israelites when they were taken to Persia and Babylon. Sometimes this word is used to describe Jews living outside the borders of Israel, even when they do so voluntarily. The words resemble each other for a reason. Could it be that the meaning of "exile" גָּלוּת *(galut)* is somehow connected to the meaning of Hebrew word "revelation"? Yes, it is possible, and this is precisely how the meanings actually connect. There are two sides to Revelation and Exile.

It was God's judgment upon Israel to send his people to be among the nations. In times past, God temporarily withdrew his protection from Israel, and they were conquered by the pagan nations. This constitutes an exile—God uncovering and exposing his people, intentionally making them vulnerable before the nations. Thus "revelation" and "uncovering" can be seen in a negative sense of exile and punishment. But naturally, there is also a positive side to this concept. God has uncovered something not seen before He revealed it to John. Jesus was exposed, revealed, and made compressible in a new light, in the light of his glory. It was as if his glory was concealed during his "exile" on earth, but now in John's visions, it is revealed in the heavens.

At the time of John's writing, most Jews were in "exile" גָּלוּת (galut) across the word, but God promised that in the last days he would gather his people from the four corners of the world (Is. 11:12). This would end the exile and the same time end Israel's exposure to the wrath of the nations. Even John himself was in exile, confined to the island of Patmos. Perhaps this helps to cast that scary word "apocalypse" in a more positive light.

We are not alone in maintaining that Revelation is a Jewish apocalyptic text. Sometimes the Jewishness of the book of Revelation is so obvious that some scholars, who do not see early Jesus traditions as being organically Jewish, must concoct an explanation. They erroneously propose that the current form of the book of Revelation has many clustered Christian interpolations (mostly in Chap.1 and 22) which were not in the original Jewish texts, but were inserted later. There is a theory that the original pre-Christian version of Revelation had no distinctively Christian theological trademarks.[2]

James Tabor writes that such presumed Christianization of the original Jewish Book of Revelation can be argued as follows: If one removes "the Christian material," the text itself can be read fluidly, if not more fluidly. In the example below, the alleged Christian interpolations to the Jewish original are in boldface type. "The revelation [of Jesus Christ,] which God gave [him] to show his servants what must soon take place; he made it known by sending his angel to his servant John, who testified to the word of God and [to the testimony of Jesus Christ], even to all that he saw. Blessed is the one who reads aloud the words of the prophecy and blessed are those who hear and who keep what is written in it; for the time is near."[3]

Although this is an intriguing proposition, which highlights the Jewish character of Revelation, we view the above exercise as futile and exceedingly subjective. There is no scientific way to determine what was added to the text. We have no ancient manuscripts that have those phrases omitted. Many phrases that have no

[2] Book of Revelation, Jewish Encyclopedia (1906).
[3] Tabor, James D. *How Christian is the New Testament Book of Revelation*, article in "Huffington Post", 2013.

connection to Christian doctrines could be just as easily be removed, and the main text would still be fluid. Therefore, this in and of itself proves nothing. A number of other considerations need to be made.

Scholars observed that the Samaritan version of the Torah reads much more fluidly than the Jewish Torah. The Jewish Torah is far more unpolished and at times inconsistent and convoluted in its presentation of events and details when compared with the Samaritan version. However, the smoother reading argues for the later editorial activity of the Samaritan scribes and not the reverse. So, in our opinion, just because the text reads more fluidly once the explicitly "Christian" content is removed, the meaning is unchanged. To conclude otherwise overstates any evidence that supposed "Christian interpolations" in Revelation are anything more than a curious and intriguing possibility. There is no known textual evidence to support this idea.

But there is another more central problem that we believe plagues those who argue that the original Jewish Apocalypse (The Book of Revelation) was tampered with and/or Christianized by some unknown person at the end of the first century or later. In short, those who hold this view fail to see that such phrases (designated by them in boldface) as "Jesus Christ" and his "testimony" (among others) are also first-century Jewish terms and native Jewish concepts that only centuries later became distanced from their original Israelite context and came to be understood as "Christian". Such differentiation between Jewish and Christian material is an anachronistic and artificial argument. Such arguments demonstrate a lack of understanding of the first-century Jewish environment, as well as the absence of any subsequent, clear-cut Christian identity as opposed to Jewish identity.

Indeed, Revelation resembles other Jewish books written in the same style. Consider the imagery of animals meant to represent humans in Revelation. In the 1st Book of Enoch (2nd century BCE) the seer falls asleep. He sees a dream based entirely on the familiar flow of Israel's history. Only the actors in this dream are not people, but animals. All of the greatest leaders and kings of Israel are rams. The leaders of Israel are also called "shepherds of the sheep". God is called the "Lord of the sheep."

> "And I saw till a throne was erected in the pleasant land, and the Lord of the sheep sat Himself thereon, and the other took the sealed books and opened those books before the Lord of the sheep." (1 Enoch 90:20)

Does this vision of Enoch sound familiar? The "other" (next to the Lord of the sheep) opens the sealed scroll… In Revelation, a very unusual-looking Lamb (who was slain) is the only one worthy to open the scroll with seven seals. The Lamb represents someone, and the readers are supposed to guess the identity of the Lamb.

> [37] And I saw that a white bull was born, with large horns... [38] And I saw till all their generations were transformed, and they all became white bulls; and the first among them became a lamb, and that lamb became a great

> animal and had great black horns on its head;
> and the Lord of the sheep rejoiced over it and
> over all the oxen. [39] And I slept in their midst:
> and I awoke and saw everything. [40] This is the
> vision which I saw while I slept... (1 Enoch
> 90:37-40)

The content of John's visions and the symbols he uses to describe what he saw were familiar to the Jewish audience of that day. These techniques belong to the genre of apocalyptical books, many of which emerged from the 3rd century BCE to the 2nd century CE.

Apocalyptical books use images, symbols, and cultural and linguistic codes that make perfect sense to the insider audience but often are meaningless and confusing to outsiders. The image of the Beast and its number is a perfect example.

> [15] ...as many as do not worship the image of
> the beast to be killed. [16] And he causes all, the
> small and the great, and the rich and the poor,
> and the free men and the slaves, to be given a
> mark on their right hand or on their forehead,
> [17] ...no one will be able to buy or to sell,
> except the one who has the mark... [18] Here is
> wisdom. Let him who has understanding
> calculate the number of the beast, for the
> number is that of a man, and his number is six
> hundred and sixty-six. (Rev 13:15-18)

The idea of the terrible Beast follows the apocalyptical tradition of animals being representations of people. The number 666 is a Gematria, a numeric code meant to help people to calculate and identify whom John is really writing about. The "mark of the beast" (whatever form or shape it was to take) was to be placed on the head and on the hand, according to Revelation. To a Jewish audience, such placement sounds very familiar and would make perfect symbolic sense.

In one of the passages recited daily by Jews devotionally since antiquity, Israelites were commanded to place God's words on themselves, "to bind them as a sign on your hand" and wear them "as frontals on your forehead" between the eyes (Deut. 6:8). In the Jewish community, these verses are practiced by wearing "phylacteries" or "tefillin" during morning prayer. Tefillin is a set of two small boxes containing portions of Torah texts which are placed on the head and arm and attached with leather straps. One literarily wears God's words and makes God's ways a tangible part of his life. The "mark of the Beast" is analogical to tefillin. This mark would also be a sign of loyalty, but not to God of Israel and his Torah but rather to the Beast and his ways.

The name "Nero Caesar" spelled in Hebrew נרון קסר (neron qesar) adds up to 666. Of course, the names of other historical people could match the same numeric value, so someone can argue that this is a lucky guess and it means nothing. But curiously, some later Greek manuscripts of Revelation feature the number 616 instead of 666. Why? The number is a name, and it was deliberately adjusted to line up with the Latin spelling of Nero's name - NERO CAESAR (dropping the "n" letter used in Hebraic spelling). This would not work with other proposed names that match the 666 sum. The Latin spellings of those names would no longer line up to the numeric value of 616. Nero's name is unique in this respect. The identity of who 666 stands for was known to some scribes. They intentionally adjusted the number for the symbolism to work in Latin.

In Jewish circles this technique is called Gematria, a literary device often associated with mysticism, secret things and used to purposely conceal something's meaning. The method is simple. In Hebrew, letters are also numbers, so A would be 1, B would be 2, and so on in a sequential system. The end result is that any word can have a mathematical value, which is the sum of the letter values added together.

Rabbi David Kimchi (12th century) believed that Messiah's actual name is Menachem. He based his opinion on gematria of the Hebrew word צֶמַח (*tzemach*) "branch" which describes Messiah in Zech 3:8.

The numerical value of צֶמַח (*tzemach*) is 90+40+8=138. Menachem - מְנַחֵם "comforter" is the name of Messiah from Lam 1:16 discussed in Babylonian Talmud, Sanhedrin 98b. It has the same numeric value (40+50+8+40=138). Based on such logic, the Branch (Messiah in Zechariah) and Menachem (Messiah in Lamentations) are the same. Unlike *Tzemach*, Menachem is a common Jewish name.

So, the Beast of Revelation is Nero? If we consider how first-century Jewish readers would treat such reference, how they would interpret what they read in John's message, then it appears to be the case. But wasn't Nero long dead when John was writing Revelation? Indeed, Nero died in the year 68 CE. Why would he surface as the Beast persecuting the believers in that age?

Our guess is that Nero became a name unto itself, perhaps like Herod became an idiomatic name used for cruel, murderous rulers even in non-Jewish circles. The war Nero presided over led to the destruction of the Jerusalem Temple, the greatest tragedy first-century Jews could imagine. And ironically, Nero claimed a divine status, expecting special honors to his name. He was a symbol, the epitome of all wicked Roman Emperors, a surrogate for the pagan Roman system and its legion of false deities, the antithesis of all that that is good and right in Jewish minds. Our guess it that his name was used how people still use Hitler's name today, despite the fact that he is long gone. He is a symbol and represents any head of the despised Roman Empire.

Revelation is full of symbols that express anti-imperial notions. But because they are presented in symbols and visions, their meaning is subjective, and only the "in crowd" would be sure of what these symbols represented. It takes a good measure of cultural awareness to interpret these unique references in such light.

Chapter 2: The Hebrew Structure of Revelation

As we continue to peer into the book of Revelation, we repeatedly see that the book is not a sporadically written account as the author was simply awed by what he saw. Instead, the book of Revelation has a very carefully crafted literary structure characteristic of biblical literary traditions in general, and of the Jewish apocalyptic genre specifically. However, those elements are combined with epistolary (letter-writing) components and a clear prophetic tone. Consider this deliberate structure:

Blessed is the one who reads aloud the words of this prophecy, and blessed are those who hear, and who keep what is written in it, for the time is near (Rev. 1:3)

When we come to verse 3, we are introduced to a series of seven blessings (ברכות, *brachot*) that are interspersed throughout the book. It is too early in our exploration to see the rhythmic pattern of John's presentation and how these seven blessings serve as literary devices that help to organize and communicate John's vision. However, a part of the pattern can be discerned even now.

The number seven is a crucial number throughout the book and constitutes the numeric base structure of the book's composition. The word Messiah (anointed one) or "Christ" is used seven times (1.1, 1.2, 1.5, 11.15, 12.10, 20.4, 20.6), John announces Messiah's coming seven times (2:5, 2:16, 3:21, 16:15, 22:6, 22:12, 22:20). Seven times the form "Lord God Almighty/Lord of Hosts" is used (1:8, 4:8, 11:17, 15:3, 16:7, 19:6, 21:22). Moreover, there are seven "amens" in the book (1:6, 1:7, 3:14, 5:14, 7:12, 19:4, 22:20), the word "prophets" is referred to seven times (10:7, 11:18, 16:6, 18:20, 18:24, 22:6, 22:9). The phrase "the one who sits on the throne" is also used seven times (4:9, 5:1, 5:7, 5:13, 6:16, 7:15, 21:5).[4]

It becomes obvious to the reader that the author is fond of the number seven and uses it intentionally over and over, perhaps even overusing it. There are other ways that the number seven is used in Revelation, usually in multiples (the name of Jesus is used fourteen times, and the Lamb is mentioned twenty-eight times.)

Sometimes seven refers to the exact numeric or mathematical value of something, but in other Jewish writings it appears to be used idiomaticly or symbolicly. Consider these passages:

> "If Cain is avenged sevenfold, then Lamech seventy-sevenfold." (Gen. 4:24)

> "Peter said to him: Lord, how often shall my brother sin against me and I forgive him? Up to seven times? Jesus said to him: I do not say

[4] Bauckham Richard, The Climax of Prophecy, (Bloomsbury Publishing Edinburgh, 1993),1-38.

to you, up to seven times, but up to seventy
times seven." (Matt. 18:21-22)

In the ancient Hebrew tradition, the number seven
conceptually represents completion or perfection—the
idea of wholeness connected to God himself. In texts
belonging to apocalyptical Jewish tradition, the meaning
of the number seven can be literal or symbolic, and it is
not always easy to determine which is meant. Still, it is
obvious to most readers that the number seven appears
throughout the book very intentionally.

At this point in our study, it is important that we survey
all the seven blessings and see how the first one (Rev.
1:3) is related to the other six blessings. Please, allow us
to give a brief explanation about Chiasm—the modern
term for a literary method used by some ancient Jewish
writers to draw attention to specific elements in their
works.

In modern biblical studies, Chiasm is named for the
Greek letter *Chi* (X) which looks a lot like Hebrew
Aleph - א. Essentially this is the way Semitic thought
patterns came to be represented in literary studies. In
addition, Jewish poetic style is based on parallelism,
repetition, and analogy. Typically, the second line or
idea repeats the content of the first line, sometimes
taking it further, sometimes elaborating or clarifying it.
It is easier to first show a diagram of how chiastic
structure looks before attempting to explain it. The
literary unit, when analyzed, has the following structure:

The sentence, either word-by-word or at the very least,
thought-by-thought, is repeated in the beginning and at

the end of the literary unit. It is as if the original author goes from A1 to B1, from B1 to C1, from C1 to D1. Then he suddenly switches gears and moves backward in the same order (D2, C2, B2, A2).

Parallelism is built on pairs, but John uses the number seven. We suggest that the first blessing (Rev. 1:3) stands outside of the chiastic structure that follows it. It functions as a *maftir* (מפטיר)—a summary statement found in the Torah. Its purpose is to summarize or set the stage for the remaining six blessings that are in fact, organized in the chiastic form. In this way, John still has a chiasm and yet uses seven and not six statements. Once we look at the entire set, the parallelism of meaning is very hard to deny. Here is how we see it:

Summary statement: "**Blessed** is he who reads and those who hear the words of this prophecy, and keep those things, which are written in it; for the time is near." (Rev. 1:3)

Each summary statement is connected to Rev. 1:1-2 where we are told that this apocalypse (unveiling) concerns events that are soon to come (in vs. 3 "for the time is near"). What makes this chiastic Hebrew structure hard to see is the fact that it is scattered across the entire book. That's unexpected! But the keyword "blessed" - μακάριος (*makarios*) illuminates the path.

A1. Blessed are the dead who die in the Lord from now on.' 'Yes,' says the Spirit, 'that they may rest from their labors, and their works follow them. (Rev. 14:13)
> **B1.** Behold, I am coming as a thief. **Blessed** is he who watches and keeps his garments, lest he

walk naked and they see his shame." (Rev. 14:13)

> **C1. *Blessed*** are those who are called to the marriage supper of the Lamb! (Rev. 16:15)
>
> **C2. *Blessed*** and holy is he who has part in the first resurrection. (Rev. 20:6)

B2. Behold, I am coming quickly! ***Blessed*** is he who keeps the words of the prophecy of this book. (Rev. 22:7)

A2. *Blessed* are those who obey His commandments, that they may have the right to the tree of life, and may enter through the gates into the city. (Rev. 22:14)

Notice that A1 and A2 speak of the death of the believer and his eternal destiny (dying in the Lord, having the right to the tree of life, and entering through the gate into the city of the New Jerusalem). John paints a picture for his readers and hearers of the gates of the city with the names of the twelve of Israel tribes inscribed on them.

Both B1 and B2 are without a doubt connected by the desperate need for vigilance (I am coming as a thief, and I am coming quickly). Moreover, the idea of keeping is also a connecting factor (keeping the garments from being stolen, keeping the words of the prophecy).[5]

---

[5] Jesus spoke of coming as a thief in the night in his apocalyptic discourse in Matt. 24. In his parables, he also used wedding imagery in the expectation of God's Kingdom – as the bride waits for the groom. Weddings are accompanied by a grand feast and one needs "wedding garments" to enter feasts (Matt. 22:11-14).

The blessings of C1 and C2 are also connected by a common theme – both speak of the blessed future for the believer (being called to the wedding[6] of the Lamb and being deserving of taking part in the first resurrection).

The idea of being **"blessed"** sometimes gets lost in translation. The Greek word translated as "blessed" is μακάριος (*makarios*), which is the closest equivalent of the Hebrew adjective אַשְׁרֵי (*ashrey*) meaning happy, joyful, blessed, and found in a favorable circumstance. This noun expresses a passive idea of being on the receiving end of favor and is most often found in the book of Psalms. In fact, the book opens with this word, "How *blessed* is the man who does not walk in the counsel of the wicked" (Ps 1:1).

Consider the following text:

> [Blessed is he who walks] with a pure heart and who does not slander with his tongue. Blessed are those who hold fast to her [i.e., wisdom's] laws and do not hold to the ways of evil. Bless[ed] are those who find joy in her and do not overflow with the ways of folly. Blessed are those who ask for her with clean hands and do not seek her with a deceitful [heart]. Blessed is the man who grasps hold of wisdom and walks in the Torah of the Most High [God]. (The Qumran Beatitudes from Scroll 4Q525)

---

[6] First century Jewish wedding feasts presented two opportunities to join the celebration. One was general admission as one simply was ready and followed the bridal processional in the courtyard of the groom's house. The other was by individual invitation, which was dispatched well ahead of time to family and friends.

If this passage from Qumran (the Dead Sea Scrolls) sounds familiar, you may have recognized the close similarities with the famous "Sermon on the Mount." The Qumran text indeed has common elements but predates the Matthew text by at least a hundred years.

The main reason for their close similarity lies in the fact that both authors utilize a Hebrew poetic style that imitates Psalms. In the Gospel of Matthew, Jesus uses this traditional Hebrew form as he speaks to a crowd of people on the slopes near the Sea of Galilee.

As we continue to move from verse to verse and from chapter to chapter, we can already see early glimpses of the level of authorial design in the composition of the book of Revelation, and how it incorporates traditional contours of the genre of Jewish apocalyptic literature. The apocalypse is always revelatory; it informs as it unveils otherworldly experiences and visualizes cosmic reality. There is a story, a narrative that can be followed. These big picture descriptions of the events of the heavenly realm act as backdrops to the events experienced by the audience of the apocalyptic writer. This is a parallel, an analogical thinking, typical of the Middle East. The earthly events are presented in light of the heavenly, unveiling the greater reality.

MY REQUEST

Dear reader, may I ask you for a favor? Would you take three minutes of your time and provide encouraging feedback to other people about this book (assuming you like it so far, of course!)?

Here is how: Go to Amazon.com, find this book "Hebrew Insights from Revelation," and write a brief customer review!

After writing a review, please drop me a personal note and let me know - dr.eli.israel@gmail.com.

In His Grace,

Dr. Eli Lizorkin-Eyzenberg

Chapter 3: Revelation as a Letter to Real People

Throughout the history of its interpretation among Christians, the book of Revelation has remained a timeless message, often connected to contemporary struggles. Consequently, the real people, the original audience to whom John wrote, were lost in the shuffle. People started to read Revelation strictly as a message to the universal cosmic church, whose truth rings out across centuries. They forgot about those early Christ-followers of Asia Minor to whom these words were announced.

Whatever interpretations of this heavenly message we may hold today, the message must have made sense to the original audience of John's day. It would be painfully cruel to give them worlds that are not applicable to them; words meant for thousands of years after their persecutions were over. That does not seem right. Revelation is a real letter addressed to real people who lived very real lives and struggled to stay faithful to Israel's God in a dark and pagan world. The message of Revelation speaks to the core of their persecutions; we must understand it in this light first and foremost.

John to the seven assemblies that are in the province of Asia (Rev.1:4)

While the genre of Revelation is an apocalypse, it is not a pure apocalypse; its message is set in the context of a letter. Also, the "book" of Revelation is not really a book; it is, in fact, a letter addressed to assemblies in the province of Asia. By its own witness, this apocalyptic letter also contains prophecy (Rev. 1:3, 22:7).

For contemporary readers, it is exceedingly common to think of prophecy as predictive. However, to an Israelite mind, prophecy was primarily a proclamation of previously known truth, a call to return to something forgotten, and a warning not to forget the important matters.

While it is not possible to identify with absolute confidence the particular John who wrote Revelation, it is clear that his identity was known to the seven historic assemblies mentioned in the letter. Yochanan (יוחנן) was a very common Jewish name. The author must have been authoritative enough to be accepted, since the Revelation of John was not the only apocalypse written and circulating at that time. The authorship of John the Apostle is early and strongly attested by several second-century congregational leaders (such as Melito, bishop of Sardis (c. 165 CE), and Irenaeus of Smyrna (c. 180 CE) whose communities were among the original recipients of the letter of Revelation). They mention that the letter was believed to be from John the Apostle.[7]

The case for Johannine authorship of Revelation ironically is stronger than that for the Gospel of John. The most significant argument in favor of another author (meaning that the author of the fourth gospel

---

[7] c. 165 CE; Eusebius, *H.E.* 4.26.2, c. 180 CE; *Adv.Haer.* 3.11.1, 4.20.11, 4.35.2; Rev. 1:11; 3:1-6; 2:8-11.

and Revelation are not the same person) is that the Greek of Revelation is significantly lower in quality than the Greek of the Gospel of John. This, however, could be easily explained by realizing that John, while composing his gospel, used a scribe, as did Paul and many other writers in Roman antiquity.[8] Perhaps no scribe was available to John when he assembled Revelation. According to longstanding tradition, the book was composed when he was under house arrest on the island of Patmos. In other words, he was left with his own limited Greek language skills, and what he put together is not of the same literary quality as his gospel. Ultimately, while the identify of the author is important, it is not as important as the message he delivers.

All seven assemblies mentioned in the letter are located within the system of Ancient Roman roads in Asia Minor. It was possible for the letter to make a full circle of all the locations after it was originally delivered and read in the individual congregations. However, not all the known congregations in Asia were addressed. For example, the congregation at Colossae is not mentioned. The letter is tied to the importance of the number seven, pointing to the symbolic nature of these churches. It is likely that the seven actual historic congregations symbolized all the gatherings which existed at the time of John and raising that number beyond seven would take away from the poetic symbolism of the message.

---

[8] Romans 16:22: "I, Tertius, the one writing this letter, greet you in the Lord."

The Book of Revelation confronts each of the seven communities with an alternative image of the world. Living in the great cities of the province of Asia, the letter's recipients would have been extremely familiar with the powerful images of Roman imperial greatness, excellence, and domination "by right." John's letter claims to reveal an invisible but much truer reality.

In Roman cities, civic and religious architecture, iconography, statues, rituals, and festivals all served as impressive visual displays of Roman imperial power and the magnificent splendor of pagan worship. The visual power of John's letter stands in opposition to that visible reality in order to "cleanse" or refresh the minds of his hearers.

In chapter 17, for example, John describes his vision of a woman. At first, she sounds like the goddess Roma in all her glory: "And the woman was clothed in purple and scarlet, and adorned with gold and precious stones and pearls, holding a golden cup in her hand…" (Rev. 17:4)

At many temples throughout Asia Minor, people worshipped this goddess as the personification of the majestic Roman civilization. Yet John turns this image on its head, portraying the woman not as some noble figure but as a murderous prostitute. Her wealth and splendor represent the evil gains of her disreputable trade.

> On her forehead was written a mysterious name: Babylon the Great, Mother of the Prostitutes and Abominations of the Earth. And I saw the woman drunk with the blood of

the holy ones, and with the blood of Jesus'
witnesses. (Rev. 17:5-6)

This image has caused much speculation. A great deal
of ink has been spilled attempting to define this woman
– Babylon. However, all one has to do is to glance at a
coin minted in the year 71 CE, a coin with the image of
the Emperor Vespasian on it, to see who this woman
really is. On the reverse side of that coin is an image of
the goddess Roma, literally sitting on seven hills.
Anyone who has ever seen this coin or held it in their
hands would immediately make this connection. But
modern readers of Revelation are so far removed from
Roman antiquity, that many fanciful explanations of
this woman continue to dominate religious
commentaries. In reality, the explanation is much
simpler.

As a Jewish apocalyptic book, Revelation echoes the
ideas of the first-century but imbues them with radically
new meanings, meanings that come from Jewish
culture. The invasion from the East (Rev. 9:13-19,
16:12) and the "beast who was and is not and is about
to come up from the bottomless pit" (Rev. 17:8) are
also allusions to Rome.

In the late 1st century C.E., the threat of invasion from
the Parthian (Persian) empire was real and widely felt.
According to a popular myth, the tyrant Nero would
come back from the grave at the head of the Parthian
hordes to conquer the Roman empire. The letter of
Revelation plays on this fear and envisions an alliance
between "the beast" and the kings of the East. History
is a powerful ally in interpreting how the generation of

first-century believers might have understood these strange and ominous predictions.

Grace and peace to you from "he who is," and who was, and who is still to come, (Rev.1:5a)

This is a seemingly simple greeting on the surface. But in reality, its an allusion to God's special four-letter name. According to the Greek language of Septuagint, in Ex. 3:14 God refers to himself as "he who is" (ὁ ὤν, *ho on*). The Greek is a translation of divine self-description in Hebrew "I am who I am" אֶהְיֶה אֲשֶׁר אֶהְיֶה (*ehyeh asher ehyeh*). John uses the same Greek wording only in this place. God's unpronounceable name YHWH is believed to be connected to the verb "to be" in Hebrew. It is a composite of past, present, and future aspects—all present and blended in one single word, "who is and the one who was, and who will be." The meaning is deliberate and obvious for anyone who "hears" the Greek words but "thinks" in Hebrew.

This passage is one of many places in Revelation where it could be said that the Greek used by John is poor. Yes, Greek does not appear to be the native language of the author of Revelation. He apparently lacks eloquence. However, it is possible that the Greek grammatical irregularities observed in Revelation may have been caused by John's attempt to translate his original thought language (Hebrew or Aramaic) into Greek. It is also possible that the awkward grammatical structures in Revelation are, in fact, intentional! For the reader familiar with the nuances of both Hebrew and Greek grammar, they act as clues that something else is going on. It's the big picture that is important.

...and from the seven spirits who are before his throne, (Rev.1:5b)

The number "seven" (שבעה, *shevah*) in a wide variety of Jewish traditions is the number of fullness, totality, and completeness. As was already mentioned, Revelation is replete with sets of the number seven. As in the case of the seven churches, this fact calls attention not to the number itself, but instead to the totality of that which is discussed – in this case, the Spirit, namely, seven spirits who is/are before the throne of God. There are at least two interpretive options here. One has to do with the Holy Spirit, and the other has to do with seven angelic beings.

A common interpretation of this verse connects the seven spirits (שבעה רוחות, *shevah ruchot*) in Revelation with the seven "aspects" of the Spirit in Isaiah 11:2: "The Spirit of the Lord will rest on him, the spirit of wisdom and understanding, the spirit of counsel and strength, the spirit of knowledge and fear of the Lord." But in reality, there are only six aspects listed in Isaiah, not seven, because "the Spirit of the Lord" is clearly not one of these aspects. A better translation (provided by the Net Bible translators) shows that the attributes of the Spirit are, in fact, pairs. One aspect is a reiteration of another, and that would reduce six attributes to only 3: "The Lord's spirit will rest on him – a spirit that gives extraordinary wisdom, a spirit that provides the ability to execute plans, a spirit that produces absolute loyalty to the Lord." No matter which translation we use for Isaiah 11:2, the connection between those verses and the seven spirits in Revelation does not line up or explain why there are seven spirits mentioned in Revelation. It's a serious stretch.

As an alternative, we propose to consider a non-canonical Jewish book (1 Enoch) which repeatedly brings up an unfamiliar phrase for God, "the Lord of the Spirits." The author proceeds to name seven of them.

> There I beheld the Ancient of Days, whose head was like white wool, and with him another, whose countenance resembled that of man… Then I inquired of one of the angels, who went with me, and who showed me every secret thing, concerning this Son of man; who he was; whence he was and why he accompanied the Ancient of days. He answered and said to me, This is the Son of man, to whom righteousness belongs; with whom righteousness has dwelt; and who will reveal all the treasures of that which is concealed: for the Lord of Spirits has chosen him; and his portion has surpassed all before the Lord of spirits in everlasting uprightness. (1 Enoch 46:1-2)

We have here an unusual passage establishing the longstanding Jewish tradition (contemporary to the book of Revelation) about the "Son of Man" figure found in the seventh chapter of Daniel. But beyond that, Enoch's designation for God – "the Lord of the Spirits" may be closely connected with the "…the seven spirits who are before his throne" in Revelation (Rev. 1:4b). While the parallel between "Lord of Spirits" and "seven spirits that are before his (God's) throne" is intriguing and deserving of additional exploration, we may also be dealing here with an early Jewish equivalent of pre-systematized, later Christian Trinity language (albeit in a completely different order) – Father, Holy Spirit, and the Son.

The interpretive possibility we want to offer is that the "seven spirits before the throne of God" may be seen as "seven key angelic figures" who in some Jewish apocalyptic traditions were serving before the throne of God. The angels are, after all, spirits and are sometimes called as such in the Second Temple literature. It is significant that the seven angels do not only appear in the book of 1 Enoch, but also surface in other Jewish books.

The names of these seven key angels (sometimes called archangels in Greek) as stated in the book of Enoch are Gabriel, Michael, Raphael, Uriel, Raquel, Remiel, and Saraquel. We cannot say for certain, but it is at least conceivable that other contemporary Jews (including the Jew who authored the book of Revelation) had a similar concept in mind to that of the author of the Book of Enoch (1 Enoch 20:1-8).

In this case, God, the seven key angels, and as we will shortly see, Jesus Christ, are the ultimate authors on behalf of whom John is writing/delivering this letter to be sent to the Christ-following congregations of Asia Minor.

...and from Jesus Christ—the faithful witness, the firstborn from among the dead, the ruler over the kings of the earth. To the one who loves us and has set us free from our sins at the cost of his own

blood and has appointed us as a kingdom, as priests serving his God and Father—to him be the glory and the power forever and ever! Amen. (Rev 1:5c-6)

In these verses, the Messiah's five-fold description is very symbolic in meaning. The first description – "faithful witness" is a concept take straight out of Torah and connected to number seven. In Hebrew, the word for an oath (a solemn promise or assurance that a witness represents) is שְׁבוּעָה (*shevuah*)—a word that tis directly related to number seven in Biblical Hebrew. The second description, firstborn from the dead, is no less symbolic. A "firstborn" (ביקור, *bikkur*) from the dead is a uniquely Jewish title, tied to the "first fruits" (ביקורים, *bikkurim*) of the barley harvest offered on the third day of Passover. The motif of resurrection is implicit in this feast and this title is used by Paul in 1 Cor. 15:20 and Col. 1:18 3) to describe the ruler of the earthly kings (1:5a). Fourth – "the one who loves us" and fifth – "the one who set us free" (1:5b) is actually "washed" in the majority of manuscripts (λούσαντι, *lousanti*) instead of freed (λύσαντι, *lusanti*). Still, some of the most reliable manuscripts have "set free". There is a one-letter difference between the two, but "set free" is likely to be the original wording.

Such a full title righty deserves a doxological exclamation – "to him be the glory and the power forever and ever!" (1:6b). This is especially so because Jesus Christ appointed "us" (presumably John, his community, and the believers to whom he addressed his letter) to be the priestly kingdom, serving Jesus' God (literally "his God") and Father (1:6a).

The idea presented in Rev. 1:6-7 is that the multifaceted greatness of Jesus Christ eventually results in the glory and power of his God and Father. Interestingly enough, this too may have a conceptual parallel in 1 Enoch 48. We read this in First Enoch:

> And at that hour that Son of Man was named in the presence of the Lord of Spirits, and his name before the Head of Days... He shall be a staff to the righteous whereon to stay themselves and not fall, and he shall be the light of the gentiles, and the hope of those who are troubled of heart. All who dwell on earth shall fall down and worship before him, and will praise and bless and celebrate with song the Lord of Spirits. And for this reason, has he been chosen and hidden before Him, before the creation of the world and forevermore. (1 Enoch 48:2-6)

In this text, the praise and worship the Son of Man receives from all those who dwell in the earth ultimately results in the praise and worship of the Lord of Spirits (God Himself). This is indeed a very similar concept to the one described in Revelation 1:5-6. The son and the Father are distinct but somehow so connected that they cannot always be distinguished.

Behold, he is coming with the clouds, and every eye will see him, even those who pierced him, and all tribes of the earth will wail on account of him. Even so. Amen. (Rev 1:7)

What is essential to keep in mind as we slowly read Revelation, is that variety of voices are being heard (as if we were reading a play). There is God, John, Spirit, Jesus Christ, Bride, etc. As in any complex composition, such a rich polyphony of heavenly sound will demand careful and attentive listening in order to clearly distinguish between the voices and appreciate both their choir-like message and the voice of the individual performers. This can be difficult as it is not always clear whose voice we hear in Rev. 1:7. However, whoever this voice belongs to would like us to be aware that the crucified Messiah will return in power (with clouds), and no one (including his killers) will be able to deny his resurrection (every eye will see him, even those who pierced him).

As John discloses the heavenly parties that commissioned him to write and deliver the letter of Revelation, he is interrupted by two seemingly unexpected benedictions. One of them is in vs. 5b-6, and the next one is in vs. 7, where we see two Biblical prophecies invoked:

> "I saw in the night visions, and behold, with the clouds of heaven there came one like a son of man, and he came to the Ancient of Days and was presented before him. And to him was given dominion and glory and a kingdom, that all peoples, nations, and languages should serve him; his dominion is an everlasting dominion, which shall not pass away, and his kingdom one that shall not be destroyed." (Dan. 7:13-14)

> "And I will pour out on the house of David and the inhabitants of Jerusalem a spirit of

grace and pleas for mercy, so that, when they look on me, on him whom they have pierced, they shall mourn for him, as one mourns for an only child, and weep bitterly over him, as one weeps over a firstborn." (Zech. 12:10)

While the various Son of Man traditions based upon Daniel 7 were already known in Jewish apocalyptic tradition at the time of the composition of Revelation, the fusion of these two concepts (triumphant and tragic) was not.

Moreover, while New Testament documents, like the book of Revelation, mostly operate within an already pre-existing set of Jewish concepts, the New Testament's genius and uniqueness oftentimes can be seen in the merger of previously unmixed Jewish concepts. Examples include the combination of *Logos* or *Memra* of God (ממרה) and Incarnation of the *Logos* in John 1:14, and the merger of The Son of God (בן אלוהים, *ben Elohim*) with The Son of Man (בן אדם, *ben adam* or *bar enosh*) in John 5:25-28. The Talmudic sages of a later era also understood the triumphant and tragic prophecies about the Messiah to predict two Messiahs, the Son of David (משיח בן דוד, *Mashiach ben David*) and the Son of Joseph (משיח בן יוסף, *Mashiach ben Yoseph*).

> Our Rabbis taught, The Holy One, blessed be He, will say to the Messiah, the son of David (May he reveal himself speedily in our days!), Ask of me anything, and I will give it to thee, as it is said, I will tell of the decree etc. this day have I begotten thee, ask of me and I will give the nations for thy inheritance (Ps. 2:7-8). But when he will see that the Messiah the son of

Joseph is slain, he will say to Him, Lord of the Universe, I ask of Thee only the gift of life. As to life, He would answer him, Your father David has already prophesied this concerning you, as it is said, He asked life of thee, thou gavest it him, [even length of days forever and ever - Ps 21:5]. (Babylonian Talmud, Sukkah 52a, Soncino Translation)

Another passage from the Talmud, which reveals rabbinic understanding of the merit-based reward of the Messiah's coming to redeem Israel, shows an alternative attempt to harmonize the triumphant, cloud-riding Messiah with the tragic, meek, and suffering servant, riding on a donkey. It proposes that the prophecies describe two potential Messiah trajectories, which will depend on the condition of the covenant people.

"...it is written, in its time [will the Messiah come], whilst it is also written, I [the Lord] will hasten it! (Is 60:22) if they are worthy, I will hasten it: if not, [he will come] at the due time… it is written, And behold, one like the son of man came with the clouds of heaven (Dan 7:13) whilst [elsewhere] it is written, [behold, thy king cometh unto thee…] lowly, and riding upon an ass! (Zech 9:7). If they are meritorious, [he will come] with the clouds of heaven if not, lowly and riding upon an ass. King Shapur [I] said to Samuel, Ye maintain that the Messiah will come upon an ass: I will rather send him a white horse of mine. 37 He replied, Have you a hundred-hued steed?[9]" (Babylonian Talmud, Sanhedrin 98a).

---

[9] A horse of many colors (similar to Joseph's garment in Genesis).

Thus, Revelation takes these two seemingly independent and hard to reconcile concepts of Messiah, a triumphant victor and a suffering servant of God, and combines them into one person, Yeshua, the Messiah who already came, suffered, and is yet to claim his full glory.

...and all tribes of the earth will wail on account of him. Even so. Amen. (Rev 1:7)

What is interesting is that in the Christian religious imagination, all the peoples of the world are mourning the piercing of the Messiah. But given the fact that this is an allusion to Zechariah (see above), the tribes of Israel are, in fact, in view here. The land (Earth or Land in Hebrew - ארץ, *eretz*) is not a standard Hebrew designation for the planet, but specifically for the Land of Israel.

"I am the Alpha and the Omega," says the Lord God, "who is and who was and who is to come, the Almighty." (Rev 1:8)

Even though it is customary to speak of Jesus as the Alpha and the Omega, there is a distinction between the glorified Jesus and the Alpha and Omega Himself in the text of Revelation, especially in Rev. 1:4 (see the discussion above). The title of the Alpha and the Omega (first and last letter of the alphabet - את in Hebrew) appears three times in Revelation (Rev. 1:8, Rev. 21:1-8, Rev. 22:6-15). In all three cases, it cannot be immediately interpreted as Jesus (though the authors of this book have no problem in affirming claims of

Jesus' divinity as it is portrayed in other parts of the New Testament).

The only case where Jesus could be explicitly connected to this title is the later example from Rev. 22:6-15, where immediately following statements about Alpha and Omega (in the first person), there is a statement by Jesus (also in the first person): "I, Jesus, have sent my angel to testify to you about these things for the churches. I am the root and the descendant of David, the bright morning star." (Rev. 22:16). The voices may have changed once again, but based on the proximity people make this connection of Jesus to Alpha and Omega.

While it is possible to harmonize the Alpha and Omega with Jesus in Rev. 22:13 and Rev. 22:16, we think that given Alpha and Omega's identity as "he who is and who was and who is to come" in Rev. 1:8, it is not so simple. There is a clear distinction between "he who is and who was and who is to come" and Jesus in Rev. 1:4. In this verse, they are distinct. Equating Jesus with Alpha and Omega in a direct linear fashion is simply not feasible. The book of Revelation purposely paints a different, more complicated picture of God and his Anointed.

The marvelous grandeur of Jesus Christ as described in Revelation, and yet his distinction from the Lord God Almighty, may be best seen against the backdrop of other Jewish Apocalyptic Son of Man traditions where the divinity of both the Son of Man and the Ancient of Days/Head of Days is explicit and yet not harmonized (1 Enoch 48 and 69). Similar allusions can be seen in those passages, and there is a lack of direct identity between the beings in the heavenly realm.

I, John, your brother and the one who shares with you in the persecution, kingdom, and endurance that are in Jesus, was on the island called Patmos because of the word of God and the testimony about Jesus. (Rev 1:9)

Once God Almighty spoke these brief words, John identified himself as the next speaker. Similar to Rev. 22:6-15, the identity of the speaker switches between the Almighty God and Jesus. We see this in the following verse (Rev. 22:16). Here John also identifies the historic circumstances during which he saw the vision and authored the letter in obedience to the Lord's command. While we would have liked to know the exact year John wrote the book of Revelation, he thought it sufficient only to write of his exile. His exile was on the island of Patmos, where tradition says the Roman government sent political prisoners. Scholars hypothesize that the time when John was on Patmos fits best either during the reign of Emperor Domitian in 95 CE or possibly 68-69 CE during the reign of Emperor Nero, when persecutions of the Christ-followers were frequent and intense.

Chapter 4: The Lord's Day

I was in the Spirit on the Lord's Day… (Rev 1:10a)

This short remark has caused much disagreement and misunderstanding among the readers of Revelation. There are three interpretive options here. The first possibility is that "the Lord's Day" could be a reference to the Sabbath. It would make sense to speak of God's day, the Sabbath (שבת, *shabbat*), in this way. What argues against this interpretation is that we never see this term used to refer to the Sabbath anywhere else in Jewish literature. In addition, if the day of the week was the Sabbath as opposed to other days, it is not clear why this would be important. Why should Yochanan stress this?

The second option (a traditional option) is that "the Lord's Day" is the day of his Resurrection – the first day of the Israelite week – or Sunday. This theory suffers similar problems as the one above. Never is the first day of the week referred to as "the Lord's Day" before this moment. If this is a reference to the first day of the Israelite week, it is not at all clear why John felt compelled to tell his readers/hearers when exactly this happened.

The third (and far more likely in our view), option is that the "day of the Lord" refers to the "end-time day of reckoning and judgment that the Hebrew Prophets often spoke about. The phrase "the Day of the LORD"

(יהוה יום, *yom ADONAI*) is used many times in the Hebrew Bible (Is. 2:12; 13:6-9; Ezek. 13:5, 30:3; Joel 1:15; 2:1-31; 3:14; Amos 5:18-20; Obad. 15; Zeph 1:7-14; Zech 14:1; Mal 4:5). For example, Malachi 4:5-6 states: "Look, I will send you Elijah the prophet before the great and terrible day of the Lord arrives. He will encourage fathers and their children to return to me, so that I will not come and strike the earth with judgment."

Thus, John's reference announces to the reader that while he is writing from a particular historic location during a particular moment in history, he is caught up and surrounded by the reality of "the Day of the LORD" (יהוה יום, *yom ADONAI*). That is the perspective he seeks to communicate to his hearers. The visions he records are rooted in the eschatological reality of the future Day of God's triumph. Just as in the case of the Hebrew prophets, John was able to speak to the present from the dual perspective of the past (the covenant) and the future (the consummation of the covenant and the restoration of all things).

I was in the Spirit on the Lord's Day when I heard behind me a loud voice like a trumpet, 11 saying: "Write in a book what you see and send it to the seven churches—to Ephesus, Smyrna, Pergamum, Thyatira, Sardis, Philadelphia, and Laodicea. (Rev 1:10)

John was caught up by the Spirit into the Lord's Day when he suddenly heard a voice speaking from behind him. John compared the voice to the sound of a trumpet. It is not possible to know for sure what sort of a trumpet sound is meant here. In Biblical Hebrew, the term for both "human voice" and any "generic sound" is one and the same (קוֹל, *kol*). Was this an Israelite "shofar" - a trumpet made of goat's horn? Was it some type of bronze trumpet also known in the Mediterranean region? It is not possible to tell what the sounds were that John heard, but the fact that he described it as a trumpet sound lets us know that the message John received was connected with how the trumpet was normally used – a call to gather and to prepare.

When John turned back to look in the direction of the voice speaking to him, he first saw something like a *menorah* (מנורה) – the golden seven-branched lamp that stood in the Holy Place in the Jerusalem Temple. The presence of the Temple menorah would signal to John's audience that his visionary experience took place (at least partially) in the vicinity of the heavenly temple/tabernacle or, more precisely, in the inner section of the temple. The idea of God having a temple in heaven did not originate with Revelation. That the heavenly temple would have a *menorah* (מנורה) as the earthy one did is only logical. We read about the existence of the heavenly temple in Hebrews 8:1-5:

> Now the main point in what has been said is this: we have such a high priest, who has taken His seat at the right hand of the throne of the Majesty in the heavens, a minister in the sanctuary and in the true tabernacle, which the Lord pitched, not man. For every high priest is appointed to offer both gifts and sacrifices, so it is necessary that this high priest also have something to offer. Now if He were on earth,

> He would not be a priest at all, since there are those who offer the gifts according to the Law; who serve a copy and shadow of the heavenly things… (Hebrews 8:1-5)

The idea of a heavenly temple first surfaces in the books of Moses. Moses ascended to Mt. Horev and received instructions for the construction of the "tabernacle" (מִשְׁכָּן, *mishkan*), the tent of God's presence during Israel's sojourn in the wilderness. As Moses did this, he was "shown" the temple in the heavenly realm (Ex 36:30), and his task was to somehow reflect the same design in the earthy structure that was displayed in the heavenly realm. Ezekiel 40 offers an elaborate vision of the heavenly temple that was yet future. The idea of a heavenly temple is also mentioned in the Testament of the Twelve Patriarchs, an apocalyptic Jewish work from the 2nd century BCE, which is likely quoted in several of Paul's letters.[10]

> And thereupon the angel opened to me the gates of heaven, and I saw the holy temple, and upon a throne of glory the Most High. And He said to me: Levi, I have given thee the blessings of the priesthood until I come and sojourn in the midst of Israel (Testament of Levi 5:1-3).

> I turned to see whose voice was speaking to me, and when I did so, I saw seven golden lampstands, and in the midst of the lampstands was one like a son of man. (Rev 1:12-13a)

---

[10] 1 Thess. 2:16 is a quotation of Test. Patr., Levi, 6:10; Rom. 12:19 is taken from Gad, 6:10; Rom. 12:21 is taken from Benjamin, 6:3; 2 Cor. 12:10 is a quote from Gad, 5:7.

The fact that the Son of Man walks among the seven heavenly lamps (מנורה, *menorah*), means that he (Jesus), as the heavenly high priest, was the source of this revelation. In various Jewish traditions, the figure of *Metatron* (מטטרון) is similar (if not identical) to the Son of Man and acts as the high priest of the heavenly temple. This temple is located in close proximity to the heavenly chariot at the base of God's throne. In one of the books of Enoch preserved in Hebrew, we read:

> "Metatron (the name means "the one next to the throne") is the Prince over all Princes and stands before him who is exalted above all gods. He goes beneath the throne of glory, where he has a great heavenly tabernacle of light, and brings out the deafening fire, and puts it in the ears of the holy creatures so that they should not hear the sound of the utterance that issues from the mouth of the Almighty."
> (*Sefer Heychalot* / 2 Enoch 15b)

The writer of Hebrews expressed ideas similar to those found in the Qumran scrolls, namely that Melchizedek is the heavenly high priest (11Qmelch). This is why Yeshua, who has no priestly heritage, can stand next to the golden lamp.

> For this Melchizedek, king of Salem, priest of the Most High God, who met Abraham as he was returning from the slaughter of the kings and blessed him, to whom also Abraham apportioned a tenth part of all the spoils, was first of all, by the translation of his name, king of righteousness, and then also king of Salem, which is the king of peace. Without father, without mother, without genealogy, having

neither beginning of days nor end of life, but
made like the Son of God, he remains a priest
perpetually. (Hebrews 7:1-3)

It becomes clear that in the book of Revelation, a
Jewish apocalyptic figure (who previously appeared in a
variety of Jewish Son of Man and Metatron traditions)
is, in fact, Jesus Christ – the eternal heavenly high
priest. This connection in Revelation is intentional and
definite and represents a blending of previously existing
traditions into close harmony with Yeshua.

...I saw one like a son of man, clothed in a robe reaching to the feet, and girded across His chest with a golden sash. His head and... (Rev 1:13b-14a)

The description of the Son of Man's clothing is
consistent with his priestly duties, though they differ
from the Aaronic priestly garments. A robe reaching to
the feet and a sash were both prescribed for priests in
the Mosaic tabernacle (Ex.28). In addition, we read in
Leviticus: "Aaron shall enter the holy place with this:
with a bull for a sin offering and a ram for a burnt
offering. He shall put on the holy linen tunic, and the
linen undergarments shall be next to his body, and he
shall be girded with the linen sash and attired with the
linen turban (these are holy garments)." (Lev. 16:3-4)

In Revelation 1:13, we read about a robe reaching to
the feet and a sash, but we do not read about a white
turban. We do, however, read in vs.14 that his head
(and then separately his hair) is described in terms of
white wool. There is some similarity to the high priest's
attire for the Day of Atonement, during which (unlike

his daily clothing) the High Priest's clothing was all white. In a much later rabbinic discussion on the function of priestly vestments, we read in the Babylonian Talmud:

> R. 'Inyani b. Sason also said: Why are the sections on sacrifices and the priestly vestments close together? To teach you: as sacrifices make atonement, so do the priestly vestments make atonement. The coat atones for bloodshed... The breeches atoned for lewdness... The miter made atonement for arrogance. The girdle atoned for [impure] meditations of the heart... The breastplate atoned for [neglect of] civil laws... The ephod atoned for idolatry... The robe atoned for slander... the head plate atoned for brazenness... (Babylonian Talmud, Zevachim 88b)

This reference cannot be taken as the background of Revelation since it was written much later. However, it shows general interpretive trajectories (as with almost everything in the Talmud) that may be traceable to the time of Jesus and earlier. Many ancient Jewish traditions existed for a long time in oral form before being written down. So at least one thing is clear; The description of Jesus' heavenly garments is intentional. The garments are in fact, highly symbolic – showing that Jesus is the heavenly priest, fully prepared and qualified to carry out his duties.

Additionally, consider the symbolism of referring to the image of Jesus as the Word of God (דבר יהוה, *davar ADONAI*). In Jewish worship, handwritten biblical scrolls are carefully preserved and treated with great respect. They are adorned and literally "dressed" in special mantles. In the Synagogue, scrolls are usually kept covered with a cover or a mantle — an outer cover used to preserve them from the elements. In more recent times, scrolls were outfitted with elaborate crowns and finials called pomegranates (רימונים, *rimmonim*). Just as priests wore breastplates, so the Torah scrolls in the Synagogue also have breastplates. Both the crown and the breastplate are typically made from precious or semi-precious metals. Finally, beneath the outer covering, the scrolls have a belt-like sash that prevents the scroll from unrolling when not unfolded for reading. Some of this symbolism may be more modern than the first century CE, but the image of Messiah as the Word of God (דבר יהוה, *davar ADONAI*) would have been quickly connected with the Scriptures.

There is no reason to expect an precise correlation between the priestly vestments in the Mosaic Tabernacle and those of Jesus. Jesus' priesthood is decisively of a different order (the order of Melchizedek and not the order of Aaron). Relative correlation can, however, be established, and it shows the general idea of Jesus as the heavenly priest. This is more than enough to connect the dots.

Ancient Jewish literature contains many and varied accounts of heavenly visions that describe majestic and exalted beings, mysterious revelations, and conversations with angels. These texts provide glimpses of future events and even of the throne of God. Many of these literary works depict a heavenly being who is often called "the son of man" or "a son of Adam." This title can be understood as describing someone who resembles a human being.

Yochanan, the writer of Revelation, employs the same type of language and presents images very similar to those found in other Jewish texts. John describes Yeshua in extraordinarily majestic terms, employing idiomatic language to hint about his nature as well as his relationship to the one sitting on the throne.

This corresponds very closely with how the image of the Son of Man is portrayed in other Jewish apocalyptic texts. Thus, if one wants to understand Revelation, it helps one greatly to notice and to study these texts and their connection to Revelation.

> And in the midst of the lampstands, I saw one like a son of man, clothed [in a robe reaching] to the feet, and girded across his chest with a golden sash. (Rev. 1:13)

This perception of a being who appears like a "son of man (Adam)" – (i.e., a person or a human being) opens John's account of what he saw in his extraordinary vision. The text continues with a detailed visual description of this "Son of Man".

His head and His hair were white like white wool, like snow; and His eyes were like a flame of fire. His feet were like burnished bronze, when it has been made to glow in a furnace, and His voice was like the sound of many waters. 16 In His right hand He held seven stars... (Rev 1:14-15)

As John continues to describe his vision, we are reminded of a similar description of an angel-like encounter recorded in another (partially) apocalyptic Jewish work – The Book of Daniel:

> On the twenty-fourth day of the first month, while I was by the bank of the great river, that is, the Tigris, I lifted my eyes and looked, and behold, there was a certain man dressed in linen, whose waist was girded with a belt of pure gold of Uphaz. His body also was like beryl, his face had the appearance of lightning, his eyes were like flaming torches, his arms and feet like the gleam of polished bronze, and the sound of his words like the sound of a tumult. (Dan.10:4-6)

Both encounters testify, though somewhat differently, that both men (in Daniel and in Revelation) wore a white linen robe with a golden girdle, both had eyes like flaming torches, feet of burnished bronze, a face that shone like a sun, and a voice that sounded like a sound of rushing waters. The similarity is indeed remarkable.

However, other than this remarkable similarity, there are also striking differences. The Son of man in Revelation is seen with hair that is white like wool and snow (vs.14). In the middle of the description, two more important visual elements are presented – in his hand he held seven stars, and from his mouth proceeded a two-edged sword.

The reference to white hair suggests another text, curiously also located in the Book of Daniel. The Almighty God of Israel is described as the Ancient of

Days who not only wears a white robe but also has a head of white hair.

> I kept looking until thrones were set up, and the Ancient of Days took His seat; His vesture was like white snow and the hair of His head like pure wool. His throne was ablaze with flames; its wheels were a burning fire. "A river of fire was flowing and coming out from before Him; Thousands upon thousands were attending Him, and myriads upon myriads were standing before Him; the court sat, and the books were opened. (Daniel 7:9-10)

We observer that some important details (white robe and hair) of the angel-like heavenly being who appears in Revelation (Son of Man) are consistent with the description of the Ancient of Days in Daniel. We cannot yet speak of a full merger of the characters, but the passages express a certain deliberate resemblance.

The Book of Enoch contains language that is quite similar to Revelation, which is why we quote from it so often. In Enoch, God is called the Head of Days (instead of Ancient of Days as in Daniel) as well as the Lord of the Spirits. In the following passage, God is described as having white hair like wool.

> And there I saw One who had a head of days, and His head was white like wool, and with Him was another being whose countenance had the appearance of a man, And his face was full of graciousness, like one of the holy angels. And I asked the angel who went with me and showed me all the hidden things, concerning that Son of Man, who he was, and whence he

was, (and) why he went with the Head of
Days? And he answered and said unto me: This
is the Son of Man who hath righteousness,
with whom dwells righteousness, and who
reveals all the treasures of that which is hidden,
because the Lord of Spirits hath chosen him,
and whose lot hath the pre-eminence before
the Lord of Spirits in uprightness forever. (1
Enoch 46:1-3)

As in many apocalyptic passages, the Son of Man figure
(*ben adam*, בן אדם in Hebrew or in Aramaic - *bar enosh*,
בר אנוש) is in the presence of the Lord of the Spirits. In
this passage from Enoch (with which John may have
been familiar), he is not the one with white hair.
Perhaps this is John's way of intentionally blending the
Father and the Son. It is hard to say for sure, but it
seems that way.

In the book of Revelation, John also sees an angel-like
heavenly being holding seven stars in his right hand.
While it is important to try and identify the symbolism
behind the seven stars, it is more important to note that
he is holding them all in his right hand. That, of course
speaks of his great authority and power. For now, the
most important point is that these seven stars, no
matter what they represent, are under the full and
unquestionable control of the heavenly being that
speaks to John.

***...and out of His mouth came a sharp two-edged
sword, and His face was like the sun shining in its
strength. (Rev 1:16)***

As dozens of artists have attempted (without much success) to recreate this image from the vision, we must point out the awkwardness of John's further description of the Son of Man - "from his mouth came a sharp two-edged sword." The sword (חֶרֶב, *herev*) was the ultimate symbol of armed strength, dominance, and victory in the ancient world. There are many different kinds of swords. Swords that were two-edged were particularly deadly because they were able to cut from both sides of the blade. Keeping in mind the literary genre of Revelation, we know that the double-edged sword is used as a metaphor here. The imagery conveys that the mouth of the Son of Man wields great power, like that of a double-edged sword. It is able to wound and to slay enemies in a manner quite similar to the Lord of the Spirits in Enoch.

> "And the Lord of Spirits seated him on the throne of His glory, and the spirit of righteousness was poured out upon him, and the word of his mouth slays all the sinners, and all the unrighteous are destroyed from before his face." (1 Enoch 62:2)

The Second Temple literature and the Bible include a number of passages which show that the mouth can be a very deadly weapon. In some places, the words themselves slay. In others, it is fire or breath from the mouth that destroys.

> And I beheld, and lo! The wind caused to come up out of the heart of the seas as it were the form of a man. And I beheld, and lo! This Man flew with the clouds of heaven. And wherever he turned his countenance to look, everything

seen by him trembled; and whithersoever the
voice went out of his mouth, all that heard his
voice melted away, as the wax melts when it
feels the fire. (4 Ezra 13:3)

The Son of Man has immense power in this depiction.
Jus as in Daniel, he comes "with the clouds of heaven."
His gaze alone makes things tremble. The sound of his
voice makes things melt as if he is breathing fire. While
not the activity of a sword, the idea is the same. This
angel-like being is powerful enough to destroy with his
voice alone. The prophet Isaiah writes similar words:

"And He will delight in the fear of the Lord,
And He will not judge by what His eyes see,
nor make a decision by what His ears hear; but
with righteousness, He will judge the poor, and
decide with fairness for the afflicted of the
earth; and He will strike the earth with the rod
of His mouth, and with the breath of His lips
He will slay the wicked." (Isaiah 11:3-4).

Whether it is a double-edged sword in the mouth of the
Son of Man, his voice that melts all things, or the
striking of the earth with the rod of his mouth, the
result is the same. The overall idea is that this heavenly
being, described by John in verse 16, is full of power.
We see this in the fact that he is holding the seven stars
and a potent sword proceeds forth from his mouth.
This is presumably to assure the seven assemblies of his
ability to protect and keep them safe.

One very important, but additional, detail is that the
sword (חֶרֶב, herev) comes out of his mouth. If we
ponder this issue, we will be struck by this small but

extremely significant detail. Swords are always held in the hands of warriors. To be precise, the sword is always held in the strongest hand (usually the right hand), signifying full control over the weapon.

The point in Revelation is not that the hands of the Son of Man are already full, but that the powerful sword described here is God's Word (דבר יהוה, *davar ADONAI*) that which proceeds from the mouth. The writer of *Hebrews*, who likely wrote before Revelation was composed, put it this way:

> "For the word of God is living and active and
> sharper than any two-edged sword, and
> piercing as far as the division of soul and spirit,
> of both joints and marrow, and able to judge
> the thoughts and intentions of the heart"
> (Heb.4:12).

There is little doubt that the book of Revelation was composed during a time of the persecution of early Christ-followers by the Roman government. The letter John sent to the assemblies of Messiah-followers was a timely one. This apocalyptic letter is a message of a bright, hopeful future in the midst of difficult and dark times. When the fate of Jesus-worshiping congregations (both newly planted among non-Jews and those which already existed among the Jews) was not at all certain, John was shown a vision of what must soon take place. Coincidence? Before he sees all of the heavenly drama prophetically enacted, he is already overcome by his vision of this heavenly being.

... and His face was like the sun shining in its strength. When I saw Him, I fell at His feet like a

dead man. And He placed His right hand on me, saying, "Do not be afraid; I am the first and the last, and the living One; and I was dead, and behold, I am alive forevermore, and I have the keys of death and of Hades. (Rev 1:16-18)

This picture of royal authority and magnificence is further amplified by the shining sun-like light emanating from the Son of Man. In Mathew 17:1-2, at Christ's transfiguration, we have a very similar description. There we read: "Six days later Jesus took with Him Peter and James and John his brother, and led them up on a high mountain by themselves. And He was transfigured before them, and His face shone like the sun, and His garments became as white as light." The difference between the book of Revelation and Matthew's account is simple – in the gospels, Jesus' transfiguration is temporary; in Revelation, it is permanent.

So overwhelming was John's vision that he found himself on the floor, struck down with paralyzing fear. The hand of the Son of Man quickly touched John, and he soon after offered John words of comfort. The Son of Man told John not to be afraid, since he was once dead, but is now alive forever. Not only that, but the ultimate authority over death itself and the entire kingdom of darkness now belonged to the resurrected Son of Man (the keys of death and of Hades were now in his hand).

Holding keys to a particular domain is a clear sign of the ability to exercise authority over that domain. Keeping doors closed or opening them restricts or allows access. In Matt. 16:19, Peter is promised the keys to the Kingdom of Heaven (מלכות שמים, *malchut shamaim*). In Matthew 23:13, Jesus speaks of Pharisees and Scribes not entering the Kingdom and keeping others locked out, as if they had the authority to do so. In the parallel passage in Luke 11:52, the Pharisees have taken away the "key of knowledge" so people cannot enter. In the *Third Book of Baruch,* Michael the archangel holds the keys to the Kingdom of Heaven,

> 1 And the angel took me and led me thence to a fifth heaven. 2 And the gate was closed. And I said, Lord, is not this gateway open that we may enter? And the angel said to me, We cannot enter until Michael comes, who holds the keys of the Kingdom of Heaven; but wait and thou shalt see the glory of God. 3 And there was a great sound, as thunder (3 Baruch 11:1-3).

Not only does the Kingdom of Heaven (מלכות שמים, *malchut shamaim*) have gates that can be locked and unlocked, but so also does the underworld, the Kingdom of Hell (see Matt. 16:18). A Midrash ascribed to Rabbi Akiva cites this tradition, "In that hour the Holy One, blessed be He, takes the keys of *gehinnom* (hell) and gives them to Michael and Gabriel before the eyes of all the righteous, and says to them: Go and open the gates of *gehinnom* … Forthwith Michael and Gabriel go and open the 40,000 gates of *gehinnom*".[11] Jesus as the resurrected Son of Man, one whose face radiates God's glory, has authority and control not only in heaven but also in hell (hades).

---

[11] A. Jellinek, Beth *ha-midraš* 3 [1855], 28, 9.

A passage often mistakenly published in the appendix of Josephus' writings, but originally written by Hyppolitus of Rome (beginning of the third century CE),[12] explains the idea of Hades as he understood it.

> Hades is a place in the world not regularly finished; a subterraneous region, wherein the light of this world does not shine; from which circumstance, that in this region the light does not shine, it cannot be but there must be in it perpetual darkness. This region is allotted as a place of custody for souls, in which angels are appointed as guardians to them, who distribute to them temporary punishments, agreeable to everyone's behavior and manners (Discourse on the Greeks concerning Hades, Dissertation V, 1).

In light of this popular idea, it makes sense that the face of Jesus shines like the sun in all its strength (vs.16).

A lot of confusion exists concerning two ideas that appear in Jewish literature, namely *Sheol* and *Gehinnom*. Most of the confusion is due first, to inaccurate translations, second, to inaccurate reading of the ancient texts (most often not in original but in translation), and third, to a blending of cultural folklore ideas from the Greco-Roman world with Jewish notions. In the post-biblical world, both Jews and Christians found themselves mired in this confusion.

---

[12] Hyppolitus, Against the Greeks.

Without going into great detail, what is called Hades in Greek (שְׁאוֹל, *sheol*) and *Gehenna* (or Hell) (גֵּיהִנוֹם, *gehinnom*) are two different places. Although the concepts are often blended, they are actually distinct. Greeks did not believe in a final judgment or resurrection, so in the Greek mind, the underworld is the end of existence. However, in Jewish thinking, Hell (גֵּיהִנוֹם, *gehinnom*) is empty at the moment. This particular destination is only populated after God's final judgment (דִין, *din*), which is clearly yet to come. It's a common misunderstanding, but these distinctions should be made when reading ancient Jewish texts where the distinct concepts of Hades and Hell have not yet been blended into one.

As we continue to read Revelation, it is understandable why John is told not to be afraid. Jesus calls himself the first and the last, possibly referring to Alef and Tav (את) — the Alpha and Omega title. But he is also the risen one, the one who is alive right now. One can see the three aspects (past, future, and present) in this symbolic statement. Perhaps this is yet another allusion to Jesus's connection to God? This phrase is similar to the skillfully veiled reference to YHWH, the one "who is and who was and who is to come" in Rev.1:8-9.

Therefore, write the things which you have seen, and the things which are, and the things which will take place after these things. As for the mystery of the seven stars which you saw in My right hand, and the seven golden lampstands: the seven stars are the angels of the seven assemblies, and the seven lampstands are the seven assemblies. (Rev 1:19-20)

In verse 19, John is told to write three things: 1) the things he saw, 2) the things which are, and 3) the things which will take place after these things. This is the very first clue that we as readers of Revelation receive concerning the possible structure of John's composition. There will be other hints, and we will address them as we come upon them in the text.

There are many disagreements about the message of Revelation among its interpreters — probably too many. Some see it all as future or yet to come, while others recognize that many things John describes occurred during John's lifetime. Whether one takes the historical approach or a purely futurist one, some passages in Revelation appear to refer to the first century while others refer to events in the future. The entire book cannot be fully explained in light of first-century events.

In verse 20, the Son of Man explains to John (and by extension to his readers) that the symbolism of the seven stars in his right hand and the seven lampstands he walked among (Rev.1:12-13) are intricately connected with the seven Jesus-believing assemblies in Asia Minor and their angels or messengers.

There is often confusion about the word "angel" in biblical texts, and Revelation is no exception. Angels are always seen as heavenly beings. Thus, every time the word angel (מַלְאָךְ, *malach*) appears in a biblical context, the presence of a supernatural heavenly being is assumed (usually looking the way we've been taught they look — with wings and long robes). But in Biblical

Hebrew, the word may also refer to a human messenger. The same is true in Koine Judeo-Greek.

Can one make a case for human messengers/angels delivering and reading letters to their congregations? Yes. On the other hand, apocalyptic literature is rich with supernatural angelic agents functioning as heavenly messengers delivering words to humans. This is a common feature of this type of Jewish literature. John clearly writes within this apocalyptic genre. So perhaps heavenly figures are more appropriate? Consider this parallel. Just like John in Revelation, Jacob in the book of Jubilees receives seven tablets from an angel. He reads them and discovers information about the future of his family and things about to come upon them.

> And He finished speaking with him, and He went up from him, and Jacob looked till He had ascended into heaven. And he saw in a vision of the night, and behold an angel descended from heaven with seven tablets in his hands, and he gave them to Jacob, and he read them and knew all that was written therein which would befall him and his sons throughout all the ages. (Jubilees 32:20-21)

As with other apocalyptic Jewish books, John's Revelation includes predictions of future events that are meant to bring comfort in times of discouragement, and especially during persecution. At the time of a brutal persecution of followers of Jesus by the Roman government, the true King of Israel - Jesus, the Son of Man and heavenly High Priest, affirmed that all those who trust in him could be confident in their future. Christ holds them in his right hand of strength and authority. They have nothing to fear. Their future is secure.

Chapter 5: Letters within a Letter

The second chapter of John's Apocalypse, or הִתְגַּלּוּת
(hitgalut) "Revelation" in Hebrew, is actually a series of
letters addressed to the churches. However, we must
clarify the language here. The English word "church"
does not appear in this text. In fact, the word "church"
would not come into regular use in the English
language until a thousand years after the Revelation was
written. The Greek text uses the term *ekklesia,* which
was a common Greek word having nothing to do with
either the Christian faith or spiritual institutions.

The term is both secular and ancient, as well as directly
equivalent to the Hebrew for "gathering" or "crowd"
(קָהָל, *kachal*). It is natural for modern-day Christians to
read Revelation and imagine it being written to ancient
Christians and early Christian churches, equivalent to
modern churches. However, at the end of the first
century, such institutions (with all the trappings
associated with modern churches) did not yet exist. All
that a modern person associates with the word
"church" had not yet emerged. A much better
translation for *ekklesia* would be "assembly." However,
we realize that "assembly" does not imply a distinctly
Christian context for most people. And that is exactly
why most English translations continue to use the word
"church" to achieve a desired religious interpretation.
But in doing so, in our opinion, the translations take
their readers further away from the first-century reality,
prompting the readers to make connections that are not
really there.

"To the angel of the assembly in Ephesus, write the following (Rev 2:1a)

As we read this letter, we should not visualize churches with steeples, crosses, communion tables, baptistries, tall ceilings, and stained-glass windows, but rather small gatherings of people who came together to support each other in someone's home, or in a public place. These were groups of Jews and former pagans who embraced faith in the Jewish Messiah predicted by Israel's prophets. Later in history, non-Jewish Christians would develop an identity distinct from Israel and would move away from all things Jewish, but at this point the gatherings of Christ-followers (even in Asia Minor) looked more like home synagogues than modern Christian churches.

The city of Ephesus was one of the most remarkable jewels of the ancient world. It had the third-largest population in Asia Minor (around 150,000 people). When the Emperor Augustus moved the proconsul of Asia from Pergamum to Ephesus in 27 BCE, a great period of political and financial prosperity for the city of Ephesus began. Years later, Strabo (an important Roman historian) stated that Ephesus was a city second in greatness only to Rome itself. (Strabo, Geography, Vol. 1-7, 14.1.24.)

Like other cities of the ancient world, this city also functioned as a religious center. The Ephesians were the protectors of the cult of Artemis the Great (Acts 19:35), a Greek mother goddess of prosperity well-known and adored throughout the region. She, in turn, was thought to be supremely concerned with the well-being of the city of Ephesus and by extension, anyone who paid her homage from any other place in the Greco-Roman world. The Temple of Artemis was so magnificent that it was counted among the seven wonders of the ancient world.

It is interesting that although no archeological evidence for a Jewish synagogue has been found in Ephesus as per the description in Acts 19:8 ("Paul entered the synagogue and spoke boldly there for three months, arguing persuasively about the kingdom of God), on the steps of the magnificent Library of Celsus one can even now see an image of the Jerusalem temple menorah engraved in the stone. This shows that the book of Acts' testimony about a significant Jewish presence in Ephesus was accurate.

The city of Ephesus also had an interesting and rich history of Christ-followers. The Apostle Saul/Paul lived and worked there, proclaiming the Gospel unhindered for several years (Acts 19:10). Sometime in the mid-60s, he wrote his first letter to the Corinthians from this city. He also wrote several other letters from Ephesus. There Saul/Paul stated: "…I will stay in Ephesus until Pentecost, for a wide door for effective work has opened to me, and there are many adversaries." (1 Cor. 16:7-9).

Luke stated in Acts 19:17 that "Jews and Greeks living in Ephesus… were all seized with fear, and the name of the Lord Jesus was held in high honor." This was in response to the rebuking of an evil spirit in connection with Judeans residing in Ephesus and using the name of

Jesus and Paul presumptuously for purposes of healing and exorcism (Acts 19:15-17).

In addition, tradition holds that the Gospel of John was also authored from this great city. This fact, if accurate, may mean that Ephesus was also the last home of Mary, the mother of Jesus. It is likely since John (the beloved disciple) was commended by Jesus at the cross to take care of his mother (John 19:25-27). John the Apostle being the beloved disciple and his Gospel being written from Ephesus are speculations and we have little evidence to be dogmatic about them. None of this, of course, changes the contents of the book of Revelation.

Thus says the one who has a firm grasp on the seven stars in his right hand—the one who walks among the seven golden lampstands *(Rev 2:1a)*

The phrase "thus says" (τάδε λέγει, *tade legei*) occurs eight times in the NT collection, seven of which are in Rev. 2–3 — the letters to the seven assemblies. The Hebrew formula "thus says" (כֹּה אָמַר, *ko amar*) in the New Testament is confirmed by its *Septuagint* use in the Hebrew Bible, where it was often used to introduce a prophetic utterance. For example, in Jer. 22:1a we read: "Thus says the Lord…", the phrase that the Jewish sages of Alexandria translated using the Greek "Τάδε λέγει κύριος." Here this common Hebrew Bible phrase "Thus says the Lord" (כֹּה אָמַר יהוה, *ko amar ADONAI*) is also used for a reason. However, "the LORD (κύριος)" is replaced with "the one who has a firm grasp on the seven stars in his right hand and walks among the seven golden lampstands." This is once again done intentionally. As we have already noticed,

John periodically blends the image of Jesus in Revelation with key references that are usually associated with Israel's God.

'I know your works as well as your labor and steadfast endurance, and that you cannot tolerate evil. You have even put to the test those who refer to themselves as apostles (but are not), and have discovered that they are false. I am also aware that you have persisted steadfastly, endured much for the sake of my name, and have not grown weary. (Rev 2:2-3)

This type of affirmation, emphasizing the difference between the authentic and the false, is a recurring theme in Rev. 2-3. This may be reminiscent of the general Israelite practice of separation and distinguishing things:

> ... I am the Lord your God, who has separated you from the peoples. 25 You are therefore to make a distinction between the clean animal and the unclean, and between the unclean bird and the clean... 26 Thus you are to be holy to Me, for I the Lord am holy; and I have set you apart from the peoples to be Mine. (Lev 20:23-26).

Just as an Israelite had to evaluate what he was being exposed to, what he was eating, and whether it was pure, likewise the questions about the purity of the gospel messages preached by so-called apostles needed to be tested and distinguished from things that were false.

But I have this against you: You have departed from your first love! Therefore, remember from what high state you have fallen and repent! Do the deeds you did at the first; if not, I will come to you and remove your lampstand from its place - that is, if you do not repent. (Rev 2:4-5)

The traditional interpretation of these verses among Christians today has to do with Jesus' accusation against the believers in Ephesus that their earlier excitement, the emotion associated with their first encounter with the Living God, was no longer present in their lives. However, this does not fit the line of thought here. If emotions or feelings were in question, then after the words, "You have departed from your first love! Therefore, remember from what high state you have fallen and repent," Jesus should have said something like this: "Feel the excitement you once had!" Instead, Jesus called them to do the deeds they once did.

Isn't that strange? So, whatever it was that Christ was confronting the believers in Ephesus about, it was certainly not any lack of emotional engagement that once characterized their original faith. Something else was in view here. He confronted them not about their emotions, but rather about the deeds (מעשים, *ma'asim*) they no longer practiced and about not living out their convictions as they once did.

The congregation in Ephesus was one of the seven lights in the heavenly menorah of God, among which Jesus the heavenly High Priest was seen walking (Rev. 1:12-13). Hence, if this congregation no longer showed their faithfulness to the one who holds them in his hand, Yeshua threatened to come and remove the congregation from its place. This is a serious warning. However, as is customary with prophetic criticisms, the warning was followed by words of encouragement. This encouragement is notoriously difficult to understand. It is, however, the wording of these encouraging words that provide us with a considerable amount of clarity about the earlier criticism itself.

But you do have this going for you: You hate what the Nicolaitans practice - practices I also hate. (Rev 2:6)

The encouragement had to do with Christ's affirmation that the believers in Ephesus hated the deeds of the Nicolaitans. You may have heard a thing or two about these mysterious Nicolaitans. In order to understand what their deeds may have been, we must see what John was asked to write to the congregation in another great Roman city in Asia Minor – the city of Pergamum. It will add to our understanding.

"I know where you dwell, where Satan's throne is… I have a few things against you, because you have there some who hold the teaching of Balaam, who kept teaching Balak to put a stumbling block before the sons of Israel, to eat things sacrificed to idols and to commit acts of immorality. So you also have some who in the same way hold the teaching of the Nicolaitans" (Rev 2:13-15).

In these verses, we see some evil deeds, namely Balaam teaching Balak how to entice Israel to sin. The treachery concerned two things 1) eating foods sacrificed to idols and 2) engaging in sexual immorality during the worship of foreign gods (Num. 22-24). These sins that ensnared the ancient Israelites were somehow connected with the evil teachings of the Nicolaitans. The issue of eating may be connected to the decision of the Jerusalem council as expressed in their letter to the Gentile followers of Jesus. While exempting non-Jews from all kinds of burdens of observance obligatory to Jews, the council did establish a concrete set of food-related prohibitions for Gentiles as well.

> For it seemed good to the Holy Spirit and to us to lay upon you no greater burden than these essentials: that you abstain from things sacrificed to idols and from blood and from things strangled and from fornication; if you keep yourselves free from such things, you will do well. Farewell. (Acts 15:28-29)

It is not hard to notice that, out of four behaviors forbidden to Gentiles, two had to do with the Nicolaitans and the Balaam/Balak issues (eating food sacrificed to idols and sexual immorality). It is important to see that this combination of food and sex-related offenses was particularly important for the Jewish Apostles and elders to address in their letter to gentile followers of the Jewish Christ. What about other moral imperatives such as murder or theft? Where they not as important to be included? The answer to this is of course not. This was not meant to be a comprehensive list of all behaviors forbidden to believers. But these issues that were raised at the Jerusalem Council, consuming food sacrificed to idols, blood, and sexual sins, seem to constitute central challenges that the gentile followers of Jewish Messiah encountered in their daily lives in the Roman world.

In Roman society, most of the meat sold in the market was first offered/dedicated to one or another deity. The only exception for this was the isolation of the Judean/Jewish community from the rest of the Roman population. The Jews had their own slaughtering rules and privileges. Most Jews residing in the Roman Empire were part of a network in which food consumption did not follow the normal route of offerings presented to Roman gods.

The writings of Paul, the apostle to the nations, include all the letters Paul (שאול, *Shaul*) that eventually became a part of the New Testament. These writings show clearly that these same issues continued to plague the believers sufficiently for him to address them in considerable detail (1 Cor.8-10). Judging from Paul's Second Letter to the Corinthians (which we mistakenly call the First Letter to the Corinthians – 1 Cor.5:9), some Gentile Christ-followers felt they could continue to consume meat that had been sacrificed to pagan deities prior to market delivery. Paul, while agreeing with them that these gods (idols) were nothing, sided with the Jerusalem council in forbidding the gentile Christ-followers from eating food associated in any way with Greco-Roman worship rituals (1 Cor.8:1-13). Having considered this important issue, let us return to the discussion of the Nicolaitans.

Who were the Nicolaitans and what is the origin of this word that we first see in Rev. 2:6 and then is repeated in Rev. 2:15? The etymology of "Nicolaitan" is most commonly associated with the diaconal appointee Nicolas in Acts 6:5 - "The proposal pleased the entire group, so they chose Stephen, a man full of faith and of the Holy Spirit, with Philip, Prochorus, Nicanor, Timon, Parmenas, and Nicolas, a Gentile convert to Judaism from Antioch." Presumably, at some later stage, Nicolas began to teach what was eventually defined as the evil deeds of the Nicolaitans. However, this remains pure speculation. We have no evidence for this conjecture except the writings of later Christians attempting to explain these puzzling verses.

However, there is another (often overlooked) option suggested many years ago by the great Jewish Christian Hebraist John Lightfoot. It allows one to continue reading the book of Revelation as a thoroughly Jewish, anti-Roman document. He suggested that perhaps the passage did not refer to the deacon Nicolas. Instead, perhaps "Nicolaitans" was a Hebraism (in this case, something originally said in Hebrew but spelled with Greek letters). What did he have in mind?

In Hebrew, to say "we will eat" the verb *nokhal* (נאכל) would have been used. We read in Is. 4:1, "And seven women shall take hold of one man in that day, saying, "We will eat (נֹאכַל) our own bread and wear our own clothes, only let us be called by your name; take away our reproach." If this Hebrew and Aramaic word (נאכל, *nokhal*) is transliterated into Greek, it can be used as a term describing the "let us eat" people. In a sense, if this was a motto, their sentiment would have been about having the freedom to eat things. What is this about? The food that others think is forbidden (food offered to pagan deities) they intend to consume. Thus, τῶν Νικολαϊτῶν (*ton nikolaton*) "the Nicolaitans" as a group or teaching could have originated from the Hebrew "let us eat" (נאכל, *nokhal*). This would make a strong connection to the context of Balaam and Balak and the incident recorded in the book of Numbers and subsequently referred to in Rev. 2:13-15. That incident is about feasting on forbidden idol food. This may be an unusual explanation, but it makes more sense in the natural Jewish context.

The one who has an ear had better hear what the Spirit says to the churches. To the one who conquers, will permit him to eat from the tree of life that is in the paradise of God.' (Rev 2:7)

"The one who has an ear, let him hear" is a Hebraism that is used on a few occasions in the Gospels by Jesus himself; (cf. Mark 4:1-20). The basic meaning of this Hebraism is this: "if one is able to hear it (לִשְׁמוֹעַ, *lishmoah*), one must obey it (שָׁמַע, *shamah*)." In this case (Rev. 2:7) what the Holy Spirit is saying to the Christ-following congregations of Asia Minor is so important that if one hears it, one must obey it.

Besides the obvious Hebraism, there is a play on words in the Greek of this verse. The one who hears is "the one who overcomes" τῷ νικῶντι *(to nikoti)* which is a form of the verb νικάω *(nikao)* which means "to win, conquer, persevere and be victorious." This suspiciously sounds very similar to the term we just encountered - Νικολαΐτης (*nikolaites*) "a Nicolatian." If the motto of the Nicolaitans was indeed "let us eat" then as a pun, this is exactly what God promises "to the one who overcomes." If they forgo eating food

sacrificed to idols, they will eat of the Tree of Life (עץ
החיים, *etz hachaiim)* and live. By the way, in Jewish
tradition, The "Tree of Life" is a symbol for Torah,
God's "teaching" or "instruction" (תּוֹרָה, *torah*) that
guides us towards righteousness — towards living
better lives. The writer of the Wisdom of Solomon
compared the righteous to trees of life as if each one of
them were a tree.

> 1 Faithful is the Lord to them that love Him in
> truth, To them that endure His chastening, 2
> To them that walk in the righteousness of His
> commandments, In the law which He
> commanded us that we might live. 3 The pious
> of the Lord shall live by it forever; The
> Paradise of the Lord, the trees of life, are His
> pious ones. 4 Their planting is rooted forever.
> They shall not be plucked up all the days of
> heaven: 5 For the portion and the inheritance
> of God is Israel. (Wisdom of Solomon 14:1-5)

The Almighty always keeps those he calls and chooses.
He chastises them but always desires that they prove
themselves faithful so that they may be with him
forever, planted as trees in the House of the Lord.

***To the angel of the assembly in Smyrna write the
following: "Thus says the one who is the first and
the last, the one who was dead, but came to life: I
know the distress you are suffering and your
poverty (but you are rich). (Rev.2:8-9)***

The city of Smyrna was one of three cities in Asia
Minor, along with Ephesus and Pergamum, that
competed for the status of being the greatest city in the

region. The name of the city itself simply meant "myrrh" – an expensive fragrance. In ancient times, this was the chief expert of the city. Smyrna, like Ephesus, was a coastal city perfectly positioned for accumulating enormous wealth both because of its port and its central location on a trade route connecting all the other cities of the Roman province of Asia Minor. Out of all the seven cities mentioned in Revelation, only Smyrna survives today as an inhabited city. The city is located in the West of modern Turkey and is called Izmir today.

The city of Smyrna was founded twice. Initially it was a Greek colony in Western Anatolia (around 1100 BCE). After its near-total destruction in the sixth century BC, it returned to life and habitation under the regional administration of Alexander the Great (4th century BCE). Perhaps it is because of the history of Smyrna as having died and come back to life that Jesus emphasizes this aspect of his own life in his message to the to Smyrna. He was also dead and came back to life.

In a series of statements regarding Jesus' personal knowledge of the perilous situation of the believers in the city of Smyrna, the heavenly Priest, who is able to sympathize, assured the congregation in Smyrna that he knew and understood the suffering and financial difficulties of their community. Jesus assured these people who were experiencing social and economic sanctions as well as isolation from the prosperous communities of Smyrna that they were, in fact, rich. This idea of "things are not what they seem" will reappear many times throughout the book of Revelation. It's a trademark of the apocalyptic genre.

I also know the slander against you by those who call themselves Jews... (Rev 2:9)

The second affirmation of Christ's intimate acquaintance his followers' difficulties had to do with slanderous accusations made against them. Slander is an act of making a false, usually spoken, statement damaging to a person's or group of persons' reputations.

At this juncture is it essential not to get diverted from our goal of re-reading the letter of Revelation as a document directed toward a milieu of Jewish Christ-followers, proselytes, and God-fearers. Here, once again, the standard interpretation forces the reader to use later (anachronistic) categories while reading first-century texts. The traditional theory goes something like this:

1. The Christian Church of Smyrna suffered at the hands of the Jews.
2. These Jews thought they were the people of God but were, in reality, representatives of Satan.
3. Christians were now the people of God just as the Jews once were.
4. These Jews were not considered Jews because they were Jews by race and religion only. They were not spiritual children of Abraham. Paul made the point in his writings that "A man is a Jew if he is one inwardly; and circumcision is circumcision of the heart, by the Spirit" (Rom.2:29).

78

5. The Christian Church was now the Israel of God, the "true circumcision" and "the true Jews," who worshiped God through Christ Jesus.

There are so many misconceptions and anachronisms present in this typical (and generally unchallenged) reconstruction of what took place in the city of Smyrna. This traditional reconstruction is usually offered alongside the story of the martyrdom of the great man of God, Polycarp – the bishop of Smyrna and a disciple of the Apostle John. Based on what we know, he was offered life in exchange for public denial of Jesus and acceptance of the Roman Emperor as Lord. In response he uttered his now-iconic words: "Eighty and six years have I served him, and he has never done me wrong; how, then, can I blaspheme my King and my Savior!"

The story of Polycarp's martyrdom, responsible for inspiring millions of Christians to greater commitment to the Lord, may not be entirely historically accurate. The authenticity of this story is significantly weakened by the lack of any reliable early sources. The earliest manuscripts of Polycarp's martyrdom are dated to the tenth century CE and include many inspirational Christian interpolations. This becomes clear when the story of the martyrdom of Polycarp is compared to the account as told by Eusebius in his Church History, written in the fifth century CE. The differences are considerable. There are other issues, such as deliberate literary parallels with the passion of Christ, that are doubtfully coincidental. Moreover, by the fifth century CE, the Christ-followers had certainly already developed what could be called Historic Non-Jewish (and often anti-Jewish) Christianity. This "Historic Non-Jewish" Christianity did not yet exist in John's era. Therefore, it is doubtful that documents coming from the quills of fifth-century Christian writers such as Eusebius would be completely unbiased, especially when they involved the topic of Jews.

It's not that Eusebius' account of the martyrdom of Polycarp untrue. We simply do not have an ideologically independent and reliable source to establish the details of the martyrdom, especially those relating to the Jews of Smyrna, who the document claims led the way and encouraged the murder of St. Polycarp.

The accuracy of Eusebius's account has often been called into question, both today and in antiquity. For example, in the 5th century the Christian historian Socrates Scholasticus described Eusebius as writing for "rhetorical finish" and for the "praises of the emperor" rather than the "accurate statement of facts." (Socrates Scholasticus, Church History, Book 1.1). The so-called historical methods of Eusebius have been criticized by many modern scholars who assert that his chronology was something between exact science and an instrument of propaganda.

Our suggestion, therefore, is to leave the story of the dating and the authenticity of these materials to scholars of later periods and not to allow the accounts of Polycarp (whether they are accurate, inaccurate, or only partially factual) to influence our reading of the much earlier text of Revelation. We must read

Revelation as a first-century document that stands on its own, without borrowing insights and inspiration from later (and often-times anti-Jewish) polemical texts. We should be able to identify these Jews who are not really Jews from the text itself and its immediate context. History helps, but only if it is contemporary to John's words.

… and really are not but are a synagogue of Satan. (Rev 2:9)

For centuries the overwhelming majority of Christian translators of the book of Revelation have rendered the Greek phrase συναγωγὴ τοῦ σατανᾶ *(sunagogeh tu satana)* as "Synagogue of Satan." Although not entirely inaccurate, it is an example of the translator's ideological bias. We say this because these same translators are not consistent in how and where they render the Greek term συναγωγὴ *(sunagoigeh)* as "Synagogue." This may not indicated a malicious or intentional bias, but the inconsistency is glaring when one chooses to consider it. By inconsistency, we mean that in the cases when the word "synagogue" is positive or neutral in meaning it is translated in English as "congregation" or "assembly." One example is James 2:2 which reads, "For if a man comes into your assembly (συναγωγὴ, *sunagogeh*) with a gold ring and dressed in fine clothes…"). However, in cases where the connotation is negative, as in this case or Revelation 2:9, it is translated not as a "congregation" or "assembly" of Satan but rather the "synagogue"– something that in modern minds evokes a uniquely Jewish affiliation. However, during the first century CE, Jewish vs. Christian categories were not yet in existence and certainly not as terms that were mutually exclusive. Such polarization developed only in later centuries. So anti-Jewish translations simply follow a culturally developed bias.

If we read this text (as is normally done) in the context of Christian Polycarp being practically murdered in the mid-second century at the instigation of the Jews, we will not be able to see any other interpretive options. It will be settled. We will be blinded by our contemporary knowledge.

This "traditional" interpretation actually disagrees with what Jesus may be saying in his heavenly message. If one reads closely, Jesus says that those who slander his followers in Smyrna were dishonest about their Judean affiliation. They were actually not Jews. They only pretended to be Jews. Did that really happen in the first century? Yes, in fact, it did, and such reading would be very straightforward.

What if those who slandered the Jewish believers in Jesus (as well as those who joined them in following the Jewish Christ) were not Judeans (Jews) at all? What if they were recent Roman converts to the Judean lifestyle? Proselytes to Judaism were quite zealous. This type of conversion was a well-known phenomenon in the Roman Empire at that time. Religious extremism and zeal is very much a common characteristic of new converts to any religious movement. A Greco-Roman writer, Epictetus, who was a Stoic philosopher residing in Asia Minor at the time of the composition of the Book of Revelation, wrote the following:

Why, then do you call yourself a Stoic, why do you deceive the multitude, why do you act the part of a Judean, when you are a Greek? Do you not see how each person is called a Judean, a Syrian, or an Egyptian? And when we see someone vacillating, we are accustomed to say, "He is not a Judean, but he is just pretending." But when he takes up the state of mind of one who has been baptized and made a choice, then he is a Judean in both reality and name. So also, we are falsely baptized, Judeans in word, but indeed something else, not in harmony with reason, far from applying the principles we profess, yet priding ourselves for being people who know them (Epictetus, Dissertations 2.9.19-21).

Apparently, non-Jews pretending to be Jews were not unheard of. Though Epictetus uses his example to shame his own comrades, his example is very clear. At the very least, we must entertain this as an interpretive possibility and not overlay our preconceptions and conclusions from later theological works onto the earlier text. It is not hard to imagine that new converts to Judaism, those who were not born Jewish, may have mounted an aggressive attack on Jewish Christ-followers who were Jews by heritage. This is a plausible explanation. What specific disagreement they may have had, we may never know, but this a very plausible reading.

Do not be afraid of the things you are about to suffer. The devil is about to have some of you thrown into prison so you may be tested, and you will experience suffering for ten days. Remain faithful even to the point of death, and I will give you the crown that is life itself. (Rev 2:10)

The Messiah tells the faithful in the city of Smyrna to prepare for real suffering that was yet ahead. The demonic powers warring with Israel's God were behind the enormous challenges facing these Christ-followers of Smyrna. The testing of the commitment and faithfulness of the believers was said to be without limit. The number ten usually signified fullness, so here it likely does not refer to a single 10-day period of intense persecution, but rather a prolonged period that would be extremely difficult on every count. However, if someone were faithful even to the point of martyrdom, the crown of life would be granted unto him/her. Incidentally, the name of the very first martyr in the New Testament is Stefan (Acts 7:54-60), whose name from Greek (Στέφανος, *Stephanos*) has an etymological connection with the word wreath or crown.

The one who has an ear had better hear what the Spirit says to the churches. The one who conquers will in no way be harmed by the second death.' (Rev 2:11)

Jesus' call for believers in the assembly of Smyrna once again reminds people to act on the words they have heard. To the one who overcomes during the time of tribulation and persecution, Christ assures them that the "second death" would have no power over them. What that "second death" is we are not yet told. We will discover this in time as we continue our journey through this fascinating book.

"And to the angel of the church in Pergamum write: 'The words of him who has the sharp two-edged sword. "'I know where you dwell, where Satan's throne is. (Rev 2:12-13a)

Pergamum was a city that prided itself on several temples dedicated to the Roman Imperial cult. Pergamum was the former administrative capital of Asia Minor, which was subsequently moved to Ephesus. In the Roman period, the city of Pergamum became the flagship city for Roman patriotism as expressed in religious devotion. As with most major Greek cities, Pergamum boasted a theater, stadium, library, and a healing center of Asclepius, as well as other buildings that were part of normal life in the Greco-Roman world.

The healing center (called the Asclepion in Pergamum) was considered the headquarters of a very large network of healing centers throughout the Roman Empire. For many years Galen, the most well-known physician in the Roman Empire and personal physician of Emperor Marcus Aurelius, worked in this Asclepion. The Pergamum library was considered second only to the world-famous library in Alexandra. The Pergamum library boasted, according to Plutarch, more than 200,000 volumes. Another account states that Marc Anthony, a Roman military commander, bequeathed the collection to Cleopatra as reimbursement for the total destruction of the library of Alexandria by Julius Caesar.

Other than temples to emperors and the goddess Roma, the city held the high honor of hosting and maintaining a temple to Zeus – according to ancient Greek belief, the Father of all gods and man and the ruler of the Olympians on Mt. Olympia. Zeus was closely associated with the Roman deity Jupiter whose name means the "sky" or literally the "heavenly father" god. The altar to Zeus was one of the most impressive structures in Pergamum. The altar's stairs, columns, and sculptured sides once stood forty feet (12 meters) high. Today, only the steps around the altar's base can be seen in the Pergamum Museum in Berlin. The sides of the altar were ornamented with marble panels depicting a mythical battle between Greek gods and the rebellious giants who were the sons of Mother Earth.

Many have suggested that this altar to Zeus is what is meant by the throne of Satan in vs. 13. But there exist a number of other possibilities – such as the Asclepius cult headquarters or a concentration of the Imperial and Roman cult in that city. As was mentioned earlier, in Roman antiquity, the image of a sword (and specifically a double-edged sword) was highly symbolic. So, of this city, it can truly be said that it hosted the throne of Satan - the symbol of Roman Imperial authority and rule. Christ introduced himself to the assembly of the followers of Israel's God in Christ as "the one who has the sharp two-edged sword." If the above identification of the throne of Satan as the Roman imperial cult is correct, then it would make perfect sense for Christ to be presented as someone possessing the authority of the double-edged sword.

Yet you hold fast my name, and you did not deny my faith even in the days of Antipas my faithful witness, who was killed among you, where Satan dwells. (Rev 12:13)

Not much is known about Antipas who is mentioned in this passage. Later Christian tradition holds that the Apostle John ordained him as the bishop of Pergamum, just as Polycarp was appointed bishop in the city of Smyrna. The tradition also holds that he was boiled alive in a bronze kettle that resembled a bull. This first-century account comes from much later Christian martyrology accounts which are of questionable reliability. What can safely be assumed is that by the end of the first century, when the letter of Revelation was being written, the martyrdom of Antipas had already taken place. However, no details are mentioned in Revelation. Clearly the memory of Antipas' martyrdom was still fresh in the minds of the Christ-followers of Pergamum. No doubt Antipas met his destiny; embracing death because he was not willing to honor and sacrifice to pagan gods. Only one God can be worshiped and adored. Unlike subsequent eras, at this time both Paganism and the Roman imperial system were enemies of early believers.

But I have a few things against you: you have some there who hold the teaching of Balaam, who taught Balak to put a stumbling block before the sons of Israel, so that they might eat food sacrificed to idols and practice sexual immorality. So also you have some who hold the teaching of the Nicolaitans. Therefore repent. If not, I will come to

***you soon and war against them with the sword of
my mouth. (Rev 2:14-16)***

In Messiah's message to Ephesus, we discussed the evil
deeds and teachings of Nicolaitans. The most probable
explanation is that the Nicolaitans were followers of
that movement, dubbed *nokhal* by early Christ-
followers. In Hebrew, this term (נאכל, *nokhal*) means
"we will eat," and in this case likely refers to eating
meat that was sacrificed to the Greco-Roman gods.

The Nicolaitans in vs. 15 are related to the evil of
Balaam and Balak who used the same strategy to
undermine Israel. Balak wanted to ensnare Israelites to
sin against their God through the worship of Baal Peor.
The main attraction was the sexual orgies that
accompanied such worship. We read in Numbers:

> While Israel remained at Shittim, the people
> began to play the harlot with the daughters of
> Moab. For they invited the people to the
> sacrifices of their gods, and the people ate and
> bowed down to their gods. So Israel joined
> themselves to Baal Peor, and the Lord was
> angry against Israel. The Lord said to Moses,
> 'Take all the leaders of the people and execute
> them in broad daylight before the Lord, so that
> the fierce anger of the Lord may turn away
> from Israel.' So Moses said to the judges of
> Israel, 'Each of you slay his men who have
> joined themselves to Baal of Peor.'(Num. 25:1-
> 5)

Christ rebuked those in the assembly at Pergamum who
tolerated those who both professed Christ and ate meat

sacrificed to Roman deities and called them to repent. Messiah the King threatened them with his soon-approaching judgment, calling them to finally make a choice between the God of Israel and the gods of the Roman Empire. The anti-Roman sentiment of Revelation comes through in passages such as these.

He who has an ear, let him hear what the Spirit says to the assemblies. To the one who conquers I will give some of the hidden manna, and I will give him a white stone, with a new name written on the stone that no one knows except the one who receives it.' (Rev. 2:17)

Once again, as in the two previous addresses, the one who hears is called to obey (שָׁמַע, *shamah*). To hear someone means to obey him. He who obeys is described as a conqueror and overcomer. To this overcomer, Messiah promises something very special – hidden manna and a white stone with a new secret name. The first promise is easier to interpret than the second.

Manna (המן, *haman*) is a symbol of God's sustenance and provision for the people of Israel during their wandering in the wilderness. It is also called, "bread from heaven" (לֶחֶם שָׁמַיִם, *lechem shamaim*). When the Israelites came out of Egypt in obedience to God's call, risking their own lives, they were to go to a land that would only later be revealed. In John 4, while Jesus spoke with the Samaritan Israelite woman, his Judean Israelite disciples were returning from a nearby town with food acceptable for consumption by the Judeans (*Ioudaioi*). When Jesus told them he had food that they knew nothing about, they were confused. The disciples asked each other if perhaps someone had already brought Jesus food.

He answered them: "I have food to eat that you do not know about." (Jn.4:32) This secret food (i.e. "hidden manna") that the disciples did not know about is nothing less than divine energy that is able to provide sustenance in the most unimaginable and perilous circumstances. This characterized the soon-to-be reality for believers in Pergamum. Jesus promised this energy to the one who obeys God's words. Therefore, the one who obeys is also the one who overcomes.

As to the identity of the white stone, things are more complicated. Among the most likely interpretations that fit the context is a suggestion that white stones, inscribed with the names of the recipients, were given to winners of Roman sport races. The white stone, inscribed with a personal name, presumably served as a pass to a prestigious banquet only attended by the winners. This stone would have been received by the victor upon completion of the race.

While this is not a particularly Jewish cultural reference, we do know of many biblical examples of the use of Greco-Roman cultural references as illustrations for and by the Jews. After all, they were surrounded by non-Jews, and they were familiar with many aspects of non-Jewish life. Some may have even identified with part of it. Apostle Paul used many Roman sports metaphors to make his points (Phil. 3:12-14; 1 Cor. 9:24-27; 2 Tim. 4:6-8). The writer of the letter to the Hebrews also employed the Roman sports imagery of running a race and receiving a winner's wreath (See also Hebrews 12:1). This kind of imagery was well known in Judea, as it housed elaborate sports arenas. This kind of analogy closely matches the culture of the Roman city of Pergamum.

No doubt the persecuted believers, both Jewish and former pagans, were aware of this practice and the elaborate banquets of honor for the overcomers or winners of the race. While believers did not take part in these games by virtue of the fact that they included a dedication to the Roman gods, Christ tells them that in all reality, they have not missed out on anything. The real race is the race of perseverance dedicated to Israel's God. Whoever perseveres in this race and overcomes will receive a pass into the heavenly banquet of eternal honor.

Another intriguing possibility continues with the theme of priestly attire found in the first chapter of Revelation. The high priest's robe had 12 stones, each inscribed with the name of one of the 12 tribes of Israel. One of those stones was white – *yahalom* (it was stone number 6), signifying the 6th son of Leah – Zebulun. What is important about Zebulun? We read in Is. 9:1-7, quoted in Matthew 4:

"In the past, he humbled the land of Zebulun and the land of Naphtali, but in the future, he will honor Galilee of the nations, by way of the Sea, beyond the Jordan. The people walking in darkness have seen a great light; on those living in the land of deep darkness, a light has dawned… For to us a child is born, to us a son is given, and the government will be on his shoulders. And he will be called Wonderful Counselor, Mighty God, Everlasting Father and Prince of Peace. Of the greatness of his government and peace, there will be no end. He will reign on David's throne and over his kingdom, establishing and upholding it with justice and righteousness from that time on and forever." (Is. 9:1-7)

According to this interpretation, the sacred white stone could be seen as a symbol of non-Jews residing in Galilee who would receive light through the birth of Jesus. Could the secret here be the Messiah himself? Could the white stone point to Jesus through the *yahalom* stone that once adorned the breast of the High Priest of Israel? Perhaps.

'I know your deeds: your love, faith, service, and steadfast endurance. In fact, your more recent deeds are greater than your earlier ones. But I have this against you: You tolerate that woman Jezebel, who calls herself a prophetess, and by her teaching deceives my servants to commit sexual immorality and to eat food sacrificed to idols. (Rev 2:19-20)

The followers of the Jewish Christ in the congregation of Thyatira were situated in a very interesting place. This congregation was told by Messiah himself that he knew their works. God's knowledge of the people of Thyatira could have been a dreadful beginning of a merciless charge; instead, this knowledge justified Jesus' praise. The list of their works is long and explicit. Jesus took notice of love, faith, service, and endurance in their congregational life in very difficult circumstances.

He also praised them for increasing the level of their commitment to righteousness. Nevertheless, verse 20 somewhat unexpectedly tempers this celebration by words of stern warning.

The image of Jezebel is invoked, and it is not easy to untangle the chain of logic. For Israelites, "Jezebel" was a code word for the events associated with her and her husband, Ahab. After the split of the Israelite Kingdom into South (Judah) and North (Israel), we are told, "Ahab the son of Omri did evil in the sight of the Lord more than all who were before him" (1 Kings 16:30). He had the distinction of being the most wicked king who ever reigned in Israel.

For political expediency and because of his deep ambivalence toward the Lord God of Israel, he married a daughter of a Sidonian king. Her name was Jezebel, which in Hebrew ironically means something like "he will trash" (1 Kings 16:31). Ahab's excessive ambition for power was coupled with his extreme weakness to the manipulative strategies of his pagan wife. Though Jezebel appears in a variety of stories, one of the greatest achievements of her wickedness was her introduction of the worship cults of Baal and Ashtoreth in Northern Israel. She accomplished this through her dedication to a program of religious education and temple construction. All this took place under the watch of Ahab, her powerful and (at the same time) reluctant husband. During Ahab's reign, all the faithful prophets in Israel went into hiding. Elijah was the only prophet who had the courage to oppose Ahab and Jezebel publicly, in spite of the threat to his life. The Lord took care of Elijah and God's people, but he judged both Ahab and Jezebel with violent and dishonorable deaths (1 Kings 22:34; 2 Kings 9:33).

We may not know for sure the identity of this Jezebel of Revelation. Was this "Jezebel" who practiced wickedness without opposition or deterrence from the congregational participants in Thyatira, a real person? What she is accused of doing (deceiving people into sexual immorality and forbidden food consumption by her teaching) matches perfectly with previous negative addresses to the other congregations in the letter of Revelation. Incidentally (this will become important later), sexual immorality and worship of idols were, according to the ruling of the Jerusalem Council, among the major things forbidden to non-Israelites in Christ (Acts 15:28-29).

I have given her time to repent, but she is not willing to repent of her sexual immorality. Look! I am throwing her onto a bed of violent illness, and those who commit adultery with her into terrible suffering unless they repent of her deeds. (Rev 2:21-22)

Reading through these words carefully it becomes doubtful that this is a case of a woman who was merely sexually promiscuous. The idea of sexual promiscuity has always been a symbol of idol worship in Jewish culture. We see this clearly in Hosea 1 when immediately after the calling of Hosea as a prophet, the God of Israel directs him to take a symbolic prophetic action:

When the Lord first spoke through Hosea, the Lord said to him, "Go, take to yourself a wife of harlotry and have children of harlotry; for the land commits flagrant harlotry, forsaking the Lord." From this, we see that the harlotry of Hosea's wife symbolized Israelite idol worship practices at the time of Hosea's ministry (Hosea 1:2).

Just like Jezebel in this passage in the book of Revelation, Israel's enticer to sin was given time to repent. (vs. 21) Just like Jezebel, the woman in view (vs.22) will meet a violent death.

Furthermore, I will strike her followers with a deadly disease (lit: I will kill with death), and then all the churches will know that I am the one who searches minds and hearts. I will repay each one of you what your deeds deserve. (Rev 2:23)

Jesus also threatens not only to judge this Jezebel figure but also to judge all those who followed her. As in all the other cases prior to this, it is likely that the honoring of Greco-Roman gods is in view in this passage alongside the worshiping of Israel's God in Christ. All those who promoted this kind of worship a syncretistic appropriation of Christ into the Roman pantheon of gods and heroes without exclusive loyalty to one living God– would be judged swiftly and publicly. Everyone would receive what they deserved, both those who did well and those who did evil.

But to the rest of you in Thyatira, all who do not hold to this teaching (who have not learned the so-called "deep secrets of Satan"), to you I say: I do not put any additional burden on you. However, hold on to what you have until I come. (Rev 2: 24-25)

It is likely that the "deep secrets of Satan" taught by the Jezebel figure in Thyatira and the things that were discussed under the category of "Nicolaitans" in Pergamum and Ephesus (Rev.2:6, 15) are essentially the same. These are most probably references to the followers of the Jewish Christ who were refusing to fully commit to the Lord in the context of the Roman Empire's god-congested universe.

He who overcomes, and he who keeps My deeds until the end, to him I will give authority over the nations; And he shall rule them with a rod of iron, as the vessels of the potter are broken to pieces, as I also have received authority from My Father... (Rev 2: 26-27)

In a continual series of promises (Rev. 2:7, 11, 17, 26; 3:5, 12, 21) to the one who overcomes, Jesus promises nothing less than the authority of Israel's king over the nations of the world as was promised in the Scriptures. The verse quoted above comes from Psalm 2:9, and as we see in this passage from vs. 28, it applies first and foremost to Jesus Christ Himself (See also Rev. 12:5; 19:15). Yet strikingly, Messiah promises to share his own crown rights with those who will keep his commandments (works) for as long as needed.

...and I will give him the morning star. He who has an ear, let him hear what the Spirit says to the churches.' (Rev 2:28-29)

What is this "morning star"? There is a text that is often quoted in connection with this verse - 2 Peter 1:19 reads as follows: "Moreover, we possess the prophetic word as an altogether reliable thing. You do well if you pay attention to this as you would to a light shining in a murky place until the day dawns and the morning star rises in your hearts." To be fair there is little connection with this verse since here in Greek the word translated as "morning star" is φωσφόρος *(phosphoros)*. However, the "morning star" in Rev. 2:28 is a slightly different term - ἀστὴρ πρωϊνός *(aster proinos,* אַיֶּלֶת הַשַּׁחַר, *ayelet hashachar)*, which faithfully reflects the meaning of the English. There is Jewish text may shed some light on this issue, however. When the Book of Sirach praises priest Simeon the Righteous, it describes him in very poetic fashion, using similar language:

> How glorious was he when he looked forth from the Tent, and when he came out from the sanctuary! Like a "morning-star" (ἀστὴρ ἑωθινὸς, *aster heiothinos*) from between the clouds, and like the full moon on the feast-days; Like the sun shining upon the Temple of the Most High… (Sirach 50:5-7)

Even though the second Greek term (ἑωθινὸς, *heiothinos*) is not exactly the same word as in Rev.2:28 (πρωϊνός, *proinos*), it nevertheless is fully synonymous with it. The basic aspect, the concept of the morning star is glory. To receive it, or to be given the morning star *(aster proinos,* אַיֶּלֶת הַשַּׁחַר, *ayelet hashachar)*, should be understood as a promise of the glorious bright future, an affirmation of great good yet to come. Jesus is promising to grant the gift of the morning star to the one who overcomes. In Rev. 22:16, Jesus states that He himself is "the bright morning star" (ὁ ἀστὴρ ὁ λαμπρὸς ὁ πρωϊνός, *ho aster ho lampros proinos*). In short, to anyone with the ultimate faithfulness and perseverance of the overcomer, Jesus promises to give a glorious future. They will share it with and in Christ Himself.

To the messenger at the assembly in Sardis write... (Rev 3:1)

Sardis was located about 17 kilometers (10 miles) south of the city of Thyatira. The city was positioned at the crossroads of some of the most important roads in Asia. It lay at the foothills of Mount Tmolus in the Hermus River valley, a natural corridor that connects the Aegean and Anatolia. The city's wealth and prosperity can be attributed to its location, ideal for trade and commerce, and to its abundant source of water and mineral resources – most notably the legendary gold-bearing sands. Because of its location, Sardis was a center, not only for the traffic of goods between Mesopotamia and the Greek Ionian settlements but also of ideas. According to Herodotus, coins, as we know them today, were first minted in this great city. Sometime during the 3rd century BCE, a considerable number of Jews moved to Sardis because of King Antiochus III (223-187 BCE) encouragement and support. Josephus Flavius wrote of a decree from Lucius Antonius, a Roman politician (50-49 BCE):

> "Lucius Antonius...to [the Sardian people], sends greetings. Those Jews, who are fellow

citizens of Rome, came to me, and showed that
they had an assembly of their own, according
to their ancestral laws. [They had this assembly]
from the beginning, as also a place of their
own, wherein they determined their suits and
controversies with one another. Therefore,
upon their petition to me, so that these might
be lawful for them, I ordered that their
privileges be preserved, and they be permitted
to do accordingly." (Josephus, Ant., 16.10, 17).

Josephus also noted that Caius Norbanus Flaccus, a
Roman proconsul at the end of the 1st century BCE,
upheld the rights of Sardis Jews to practice their
religion, including the right to donate to the Temple in
Jerusalem – an extra-ordinary privilege indeed
(Josephus, Ant. 16.6, 6). During this time, Sardis
remained an important city and was the principal center
of a judicial district that included almost 30 Lydian and
Phrygian settlements. The Roman historian Tacitus
reports that an earthquake nearly destroyed the city in
17 CE:

"That same year twelve famous cities of Asia
fell by an earthquake in the night, so that the
destruction was all the more unforeseen and
fearful… The calamity fell most fatally on the
inhabitants of Sardis, and it attracted to them
the largest share of sympathy." (Tacitus, 2.47)

The city protected its wealth in a citadel on an acropolis
atop a fortified hill that rose approximately 500 meters,
about a third of a mile above the ground level. Steep
cliffs surrounded the city on three sides, and there was
only one access point, a narrow neck of land to the

south. Because of its natural defensibility, the city was called "Sardis, the Impregnable."

Cyrus of Persia was the first to successfully overcome the stronghold in 547 BCE. While falling asleep at the soldier's post in Sardis, a soldier accidentally dropped his helmet. Thinking he was unobserved, he went down through a secret path to pick up the helmet. When the Persians who were watching the city from all sides saw the man and the path he revealed, they were easily able to follow that same path. This later led to the sacking of the city.

Three hundred years later, in 214 BCE, Sardis was again captured similarly by the army of Antiochus the Great of Syria. His men scaled the wall at the steepest point and found it unguarded at the top. It is ironic that while the people of Sardis slept in imagined safety, conquering soldiers came suddenly, took control, and plundered the city of Sardis.

It seems that Revelation connects the histories and characters of each city it addresses and draws parallels to the people who populated them. For the most part, we look at the cities in which we reside as unconnected from our character. People have not tied the cities in which they live in some powerful way. Yet, in the minds of the ancients, this was not the case. The congregations were intricately connected to their cities, and their histories were often similar to the cities' histories and chief characteristics. Perhaps this is so because the cities of the ancients were not like today's cities; they were religious institutions that needed to be thoroughly redeemed by redirecting their worship to the God of Israel in Jesus instead of to the pagan Roman deities.

MY REQUEST

Dear reader, may I ask you for a favor? Would you take three minutes of your time and provide encouraging feedback to other people about this book (assuming you like it so far, of course!)?

Here is how: Go to Amazon.com, find this book "Hebrew Insights from Revelation," and write a brief customer review!

After writing a review, please drop me a personal note and let me know - dr.eli.israel@gmail.com.

In His Grace,

Dr. Eli Lizorkin-Eyzenberg

He who has the seven Spirits of God and the seven stars, says this: 'I know your deeds, that you have a name that you are alive, but you are dead. Wake up, and strengthen the things that remain, which

were about to die; for I have not found your deeds
completed in the sight of My God. So remember
what you have received and heard; and keep it, and
repent. Therefore, if you do not wake up, I will
come like a thief, and you will not know at what
hour I will come to you. (Rev 3:3-3)

Jesus levels one of his harshest criticisms yet against
this congregation of his followers in this great city of
Sardis. He states that he is well aware of their deeds
(most likely their financial generosity towards others
was in view here) but announces that their good
reputation (presumably among other congregations)
was nothing more than a smokescreen that did not
impress the God of Israel. Their spiritually strong,
impregnable reputation did not at all correspond to the
inner reality that Messiah the heavenly Priest was able
to see in the general clutter of their so-called
accomplishments.

We can clearly see that the author of the book of
Revelation continued to see and portray Jesus as the
High Priest (כוהן גדול, *kohein gadol*) who examines the
offerings people brought looking to see if they were
perfect and therefore acceptable for worship. If not, the
offerings needed to be discarded. He rejected the
offering of the lives of the believers in Sardis as
unacceptable.

We do not know exactly what deeds are being referred
to in this passage, but no doubt, given their incredible
wealth, they took part in generous relief to the poor of
the region. They may have been behind much of the
funding that the first-century followers of Jesus

distributed to those in need. Yet other issues, most likely the worship of local and imperial deities, had effectively polluted the offering they were seeking to present to the God of Israel in the Jewish Christ.

The call to wake up, to remember, to hear, and obey that which was received was issued by the High Priest of the Heavenly Temple – Yeshua (Jesus). This seems to be reminiscent of a sudden earthquake or of the surprise conquests of the city of Sardis. Jesus warned them of impending judgment on the one hand, and on the other, the hope of a turnaround.

It is here that the centrality of the exclusive oneness of God in worship is paramount. The שמע ישראל "Shema Israel" (Hear, O, Israel, the Lord our God, the Lord is One (Deut. 6:4) was not a peripheral concept for the Jews/Israelites. Indeed, it was also a central one to the Jewish Christ-follower who authored the book of Revelation, and by implication, also to the audience to whom he was told to send this letter. If we take our earlier observation that the biggest issue for all the other congregations had to do with the worship of the pagan deities, it would be logical to see that the things Jesus tells the believers in Sardis also have to do with similar challenges that deal with purity of worship. Israel's God alone must be worshiped. For his worshipers, there can be no other gods.

But you have a few people in Sardis who have not soiled their garments; and they will walk with Me in white, for they are worthy. (Rev 3:4)

The book of Revelation and its author seems to be positively preoccupied with the central ideas of Israelite purity (טָהֳרָה, *taharah*). We repeatedly notice this commitment to purity throughout the book. If Revelation can be called Jewish, or more accurately a first-century Israelite document, then it is hardly surprising that it has a deep concern for ritual purity. Purity was central to Israelite society since the days of Moses. The imagery of white robes, whether connected with the Israelite Essene movement or not, shows the importance of this purity requirement and commitment. In summarizing his wisdom, King Solomon encourages the young men of Israel to make life count and to do the following:

> "Go then, eat your bread in happiness and drink your wine with a cheerful heart; for God has already approved your works. Let your clothes be white all the time and let not oil be lacking on your head" (Ecc. 9:7–8).

This reference, although considerably prior to the time of the writings of the letter of Revelation, nevertheless shows clearly that wearing white clothing was present in Ancient Israel. In a much later Jewish apocalyptic work, 4 Ezra, we read:

> Those who have departed from the shadow of this age have received glorious garments from the Lord. Take again your full number, O Zion, and conclude the list of your people who are clothed in white, who have fulfilled the Torah of the Lord (4 Ezra 2:39-41).

It is probable that such traditions found particular expressions in the nationwide Essene movement with their distinctive dress code. They, unlike others, always wore white in the same way as did the Greek Pythagorean philosophers, according to Josephus.[13] In both the Israelite and Greco-Roman psyche there was an association between color white (לָבָן, *lavan*) and purity (טָהֳרָה, *taharah*). White clothes make it very easy to see the tiniest stains and are hard to keep clean. This then determines whether one has somehow been stained or polluted.

The believers in Sardis, as far as Jesus saw it, were dressed in white and yet most had stained clothing that rendered them unfit for the service of Jesus' God. They, therefore could not walk where Jesus did (Rev. 3:2b). Remember that Jesus walked in the midst of the heavenly Menorah – the seven-branched lampstand located in the heavenly Tabernacle. To walk before God where Jesus walks, to serve Him in rightful purity, required unstained white clothing. Of all the many followers of Christ, few managed to live and work in Sardis in a way that Christ the heavenly High Priest judged as right and true, and therefore as a sacrifice acceptable before the Father.

He who overcomes will thus be clothed in white garments; and I will not erase his name from the book of life, and I will confess his name before My Father and before His angels. He who has an ear,

---

[13] Josephus, Jewish Wars 2.119-161, Antiquities of the Jews, 15.371.

let him hear what the Spirit says to the assemblies.'
(Rev 3:5-6)

Once again, the reward (white garments) is promised
for overcoming (avoiding the worship of pagan gods in
favor of Israel's God alone). It was extremely difficult
to remain undefiled, given the socio-religious pressures
in Roman Empire for Christ-followers. It was especially
difficult if these were gentiles who were part of the
Jewish coalition that had not joined the Jews through
proselyte conversion. Because of this, Jesus declared
that the names of those who do overcome would
remain on the list of the Book of Life (ספר חיים, *sefer
chaiim*) in perpetuity.

There is a fascinating story in the Talmud. Four notable
Jews, respected scholars in their day, ascended to
Paradise (Pardes). Each of them encountered an angel
called Metatron (מטטרון). He was pictured in Paradise,
sitting down to record the merits of Israel in a special
remembrance scroll. (Babylonian Talmud, Haggigah
14b-15a) They each observed this angel documenting
details of people's lives and keeping records. Each
reacted differently to what they saw, and ultimately
struggled to understand what they saw, even going mad.

In the Book of Daniel, while the prophet was
contemplating an incredible vision of four heavenly
beings, he suddenly saw a similar yet alternate scene. He
wrote about it as follows in chapter seven.

> "While I was watching, thrones were set up,
> and the Ancient of Days took his seat. His
> attire was white like snow; the hair of his head

was like lamb's wool. His throne was ablaze
with fire and its wheels were all aflame. A river
of fire was streaming forth and proceeding
from his presence. Many thousands were
ministering to him; many tens of thousands
stood ready to serve him. The court convened
and the books were opened." (Dan. 7:9-10)

This idea that somewhere in heaven, there exists a permanent registration of people's names and their deeds is well attested throughout both the Hebrew Bible and the New Testament. Here are a few pertinent examples: "'But now, if you will forgive their sin…, but if not, wipe me out from the book that you have written.' The Lord said to Moses, 'Whoever has sinned against me—that person I will wipe out of my book'" (Ex. 32:32-33). "May they be blotted out of the book of life and may they not be recorded with the righteous" (Ps. 69:28).

Shaul (Paul) refers to his co-workers, "Yes, and I ask you, my true companion, help these women since they have contended at my side in the cause of the gospel, along with Clement and the rest of my co-workers, whose names are in the book of life" (Phil. 4:3). In instructing his disciples about their priorities, Yeshua taught: "…do not rejoice that the spirits submit to you, but rejoice that your names stand written in heaven" (Luke 10:20).

The address to the assembly in Sardis, as in the case with all the other congregations, ends with the fitting exhortation that the one who hears this message must obey it (3:6). The repetition may seem redundant, but this is a serious matter.

"And to the messenger of the assembly in Philadelphia write: (Rev 3:7)

Philadelphia stood on a low and yet easily defended hill at the foot of Mt. Tmolus, commanding the extensive and fertile territory of the Hermus River. The city was located roughly 45 kilometers (25 miles) east of Smyrna, 15 kilometers (9 miles) southwest of Sardis, and 20 kilometers (12 miles) northwest of Laodicea. According to one account, it was originally established by King Attalus II Philadelphus of Pergamum in 189 BCE, although another account ascribes its founding to Ptolemy Philadelphus (Theocr., xvii.88). Together with Sardis, Pergamum, Ephesus, and Smyrna, Philadelphia was part of the Roman province of Lydia.

The city was founded with the expressed purpose of becoming an outpost of Hellenism (Greek culture and language). This outpost was meant to impact the provinces of Lydia and Phrygia and establish a new frontier for the bettering of the region (Hellenization). We can see that the city succeeded in its mission because by 19 CE, the Lydians were already fully conversant in Greek and, according to ancient reports, they had already forgotten their ancestral language. The spread of Greek culture to the city of Philadelphia had come in a peaceful and extremely successful way. Indeed, it was a Hellenistic frontier success story.

Because of its fruitful land as well as other factors, this area was known throughout the Empire for its export of fine wines. However, in 17 CE, a powerful earthquake had seriously damaged almost all the cities of Asia Minor (Tacitus, Annals ii.47). Philadelphia was also very badly damaged. For many years following the earthquake, the residents felt weaker earth tremors. Strabo wrote, "Philadelphia has no trustworthy walls, but daily in one direction or another they keep tottering and falling apart." He was astonished that a city had been founded in such a place and questioned the sanity of its citizens who kept returning to it and repeatedly repopulating it.

Especially after 17 CE, life in Philadelphia was characterized by an atmosphere of constant insecurity. Most of the population lived outside the city in huts. The people feared to even walk on the city streets lest they should be killed by falling masonry. Those who still dared to live in the city were reckoned mad; they spent their time propping up periodically shaking buildings and frequently fleeing to the open spaces for safety. Those days in Philadelphia were never completely forgotten, and the residents subconsciously waited for ground tremors, ready to flee for their lives to the open spaces outside the city.

When the famed earthquake devastated the city, Emperor Tiberius was as generous to Philadelphia as he had been to Sardis. In gratitude, the city council changed its name to *Neocaesarea* (the new city of Caesar). Later, in the days of Emperor Vespasian, Philadelphia changed its name yet again to Flavia. This was done to reflect the connection between it and its new imperial patron's family name (Flavius). With time, however, the city again became known by its original name of Philadelphia.

Almost nothing is known about the Jewish community in Philadelphia. The only thing that can perhaps be implied is that it was not very different from the Jewish community of Smyrna, about which we know slightly more. These are the two congregations (Smyrna and Philadelphia) to whom Jesus speaks words confirming their true identity, disavows the claims of their non-Jewish persecutors, and accuses those who act as if they were of Judean origin (Rev. 2:9b; 3:9).

What is very interesting is that these are the only two congregations from the list of seven that receive all praise and no criticism. In his addresses to these assemblies, Yeshua (Jesus) also refers to the congregation of Satan, which is not of Judean/Jewish identity. So let us explore the message the High Priest of the heavenly temple had for the congregation in Philadelphia.

He who is holy, who is true, who has the key of David, who opens, and no one will shut, and who shuts and no one open says this: (Rev 3:7)

Christ describes himself as holy (קָדוֹשׁ, *kadosh*), or as the wholly other who is true. We should see this description in light of the reference to his having the key of David and as the one who is able to open and close in such a way that no one would be able to reverse the action. A key (מַפְתֵּחַ, *mafteach*) is a symbol of authority.

In Isaiah 22 we read of Shebna (22:15), who was in charge of the household and yet whom the Lord had planned to depose (22:18-19). Instead of Shebna the imposter, the Lord God of Israel says that he will call upon his servant Eliakim, the son of Hilkiah. We read in Isaiah:

> Then it will come about in that day, that I will summon My servant Eliakim the son of Hilkiah, and I will clothe him with your tunic and tie your sash securely about him. I will entrust him with your authority, and he will become a father to the inhabitants of Jerusalem and to the house of Judah. Then I will set the key of the house of David on his shoulder; when he opens no one will shut, when he shuts no one will open. I will drive him like a peg in a firm place, and he will become a throne of glory to his father's house. (Isaiah 22:20-23)

King Yeshua claims here that the ultimate fulfillment of God's words to Eliakim finds their realization in Christ himself. He is the one who is holy and true, he is the one who carries the key of the house of David on his shoulder. His authority to open and close is both ultimate and firm.

'I know your deeds. Behold, I have put before you an open door which no one can shut, because you have a little power, and have kept My word, and have not denied My name. (Rev 3:8)

Once Christ stated that he kept a close check on the life of the congregation in Philadelphia, he proceeded to say that, using the key of David, he was going to open a door for them that no one would be able to shut.

In Acts 15, we read about an internal Jewish debate among the disciples of Jesus dealing with a question of whether Jewish life rules encapsulated in the Sinai covenant should be required of the former pagan followers of the Jewish Messiah. After an extensive discussion, Jacob, brother of Jesus, rules as follows:

> "Brethren, listen to me. Simeon has related how God first concerned Himself about taking from among the Gentiles a people for His name. With this the words of the Prophets agree, just as it is written, 'After these things I will return, and I will rebuild the tent of David which has fallen and I will rebuild its ruins, I will restore it, so that the rest of mankind may seek the Lord, and all the Gentiles who are called by My name., says the Lord, who makes these things known from the long ago" (Acts 15:13-18).

The conversion of Roman pagans to Israel's God, according to Acts 15, constitutes nothing less than the rebuilding of David's tent as God's house for all nations. The above quotation in Acts 15 is taken directly from Amos 9:11, but in Isaiah, another text with the same idea of David's tent is also referred to. We read:

> "A throne will ever be established in loving kindness, and a judge will sit on it in faithfulness in the tent of David; moreover, he will seek justice and be prompt in righteousness." (Isaiah 16:5)

In other words, the prophets of old imagined a time in the future when the house of David "tent of David" (משכן דוד, *mishkan David*) would be merged with the house of God and would be open to all the nations of the earth. The ultimate Davidic servant of God would rule over them in justice and righteousness.

By drawing this connection, Jesus, therefore, affirmed that this time had already come – He will open the door for the congregation in Philadelphia that no one could shut - it will be the door that welcomes gentile followers of the Jewish Christ into the tent of David. Their testimony is powerful: even though they have little strength, they have kept the word of Christ and, despite incredible pressures, did not deny the name of Christ. To hear this from the lips of the King of Kings and Lord of Lords himself is a joy.

Behold, I will cause those of the synagogue of Satan, who say that they are Jews and are not, but lie—I will make them come and bow down at your feet, and make them know that I have loved you. (Rev 3:9)

To use a phrase that "this is one of the most misunderstood verses in the entire Bible" is to use a cliché, but in this case, the claim is actually true. The traditional interpretation (though slightly simplified) is as follows: The Jews, because of their unbelief and rejection of Jesus, are no longer Jews spiritually, they are the Synagogue of Satan, but the Christians are now spiritual Jews. There will come a day when persecuted Christians will be triumphant, and the unbelieving Jews will submit to them. God will make it abundantly clear to all that He was always on the side of the Christians. The Jews simply lied about their identity all these years. The Church has now become what Israel once was, God's own people.

It is clear that our oversimplified but fairly accurate summary of the typical interpretation of these texts is an example of "replacement theology" or "supersessionism" at work. We offered it here on purpose. If not this, what should be the proper reading of this text? Here are several factors to consider:

First, συναγωγῆς translated here as a "synagogue" is known today as a distinctly Jewish institution, but in antiquity, this was a neutral word used for assemblies of all sorts, secular, and religions, Jewish or pagan. Today, however, the perception is that Synagogue is something Jewish, yet such was not the case in the first century. The wordy Synagogue really did mean something like a "meeting" or an "assembly," and it's not even a Hebrew word, but a Greek one. Jews eventually adopted this term into their vernacular, but not universally. So, while the "Synagogue of Satan" evokes a clear affiliation with the religion we today call Judaism an "assembly of the adversary," is how it should be understood. Does such assembly have anything to do with Jewish people? That's debatable. The "assembly of the adversary" can denote any gathering.

Second, Jesus actually told the Philadelphian believers that people who were saying and doing these things were not Jews. Stop and think about it for a moment. The only way to twist that text to these people (whoever they are) being Jews is to elaborate profusely and introduce some outside contexts unrelated to this original message. If we do not accept the traditional interpretation that the ethnic Jews are not spiritual Jews, we could accept what may be called the plain meaning of Jesus' words, namely that the people opposing them were not Jews at all. If they were not Jews, who were they? They are most likely pagans or ex-pagans who just embarked on the path of becoming Jews. That is our theory.

In fact, the attraction of pagans to Jewish beliefs was so noticeable that Rome perceived it as a threat. Famous scholar Menachem Stern noted: "Regarding at least two, and possibly all three of the expulsions of Jews from ancient Rome [in 139 B.C.E., 19 B.C.E., and 41 C.E.], the events were linked to the diffusion of the Jewish faith among non-Jews." Ancient historians wrote that prominent Roman families had come under the influence of Judean customs. The third expulsion, ordered by Emperor Claudius, reportedly stemmed from political subversiveness: "He banished from Rome all the Jews, who were continually making disturbances at the instigation of one Chrestus." (Suetonius, Divus Claudius, 25)

Several scholars have proposed that "Chrestus" (a common name) was a Roman misinterpretation of "Christos" (a Greek term for the Messiah). It is even possible that the Roman authorities, unfamiliar as they usually were with Jewish ways, misunderstood the widespread commotion among Jews and God-fearers about Jesus. Romans may have thought that the Jews of the Empire were sparking a rebellion in the name of "Chrestus." The Book of Acts also reports the expulsion of Jews by Claudius:

> "After these things, he [Paul] left Athens and came to Corinth. There he found a Jew named

Aquila, a native of Pontus, who had recently come from Italy with his wife Priscilla, because Claudius had ordered all Jews to leave Rome." (Acts 18:1-2)

The attested attraction of non-Jews to Jewish ways in the Roman Empire suggests some interpretive possibilities for Revelation's mention of people who only claimed to be Jews. The seven assemblies of Asia Minor were made up of a large number of God-fearers, non-Jews (former pagans) who had joined the faith of Israel through their recognition of Jesus as the Messiah. Their assemblies included those Israelites who had earlier followed Jesus as the Messiah, but as the movement was growing in non-Jewish cities, Jews would always be a minority in such assemblies.

It is likely that the non-conversion prescriptions decreed in Acts 15:29 were to blame for the identity confusion and these confrontations. The group of people, led by overzealous converts to Jewish ancestral ways of life and who, until recently, were not members of the Jewish people, were most likely the ones behind the persecution of believers in Philadelphia. They would strongly object to the vision of Gentiles joining the Jewish people without formal proselyte conversion, which was not required by the Jerusalem council (Acts 15:29) and which the Apostle Paul clearly forbade (1 Cor. 7:17-24). Jesus promised these non-Jews caught in between traditional categories full recognition. In John's vision, he promised to publicly approve them (Rev. 3:9b). And he praised them for doing well.

Because you have kept the word of My perseverance, I also will keep you from the hour of testing, that hour which is about to come upon the whole world, to test those who dwell on the earth. (Rev 3:10)

Not everyone who reads these words realizes that Jews in the Roman Empire were not numerous and that they were a privileged minority. They were formally exempted from participation in pagan sacrifices and worship rights organized in each city. Since the followers of Jewish Christ from among the nations were instructed against proselyte conversion to Judaism, they were at odds with both the prevailing Roman culture and the majority of Jews who did not understand why they counted themselves among the people of Israel's God without officially joining the people. This was the primary meaning of conversion in late antiquity. Religious identity, family identity, and national identity were all tied into one. Jesus promised these precious believers that, since they had kept his commandments in spite of enormous difficulties, he, in turn, would preserve them through the hours of great difficulty that were soon coming.

I am coming quickly; hold fast what you have, so that no one will take your crown. He who overcomes, I will make him a pillar in the temple of My God, and he will not go out from it anymore; and I will write on him the name of My God, and the name of the city of My God, the new Jerusalem, which comes down out of heaven from My God, and My new name. He who has an ear, let him hear what the Spirit says to the churches. (Rev 3:11-13)

In the Roman Empire, Jews, even Jesus-following Jews, were a minority who were protected by Roman law. However, Gentile followers of the Jewish Christ were not protected. Former Roman pagans, who joined this Jewish coalition under Jesus without actual conversion to Jewish ancestral traditions and way of life, were vulnerable to attacks of their enemies on both sides – the Roman pagans that despised them and the former Roman pagans who went through proselyte conversion to Judaism (those who say "they are Jews but are not" in Rev.3:9).

Even with the promise of preservation (Rev. 3:10), the coming persecution and survival or overcoming the adversity would not be easy. Once it was accomplished, however, the rewards of the Kingdom for Gentile members of this Jewish Jesus coalition would be great. The world governments will be no more, and their laws would be void. Members from among the nations of the world who joined Jesus movement not as Jews, but as members of the nations, would be fully brought in and treated as first-class citizens of the Kingdom of Israel's God.

"To the messenger of the assembly in Laodicea write: The Amen, the faithful and true Witness, the Beginning of the creation of God, says this: (Rev 3:14)

As we can see in Jesus' last message to the key congregations in Asia Minor, he is being described in terms of something trustworthy Amen (אָמֵן, *amen*), but also loyal (faithful) and reliable (true witness). The very last reference to Jesus Christ being the beginning of the creation of God should be taken to refer to the Jewish concept of Logos or Memrah (ממרה, *memrah*) that is present in a dominant way in John 1. Let us briefly summarize the main points that are important to understand this key connection.

It has long been mistakenly thought that the ideas expressed in John's prologue are unique to Christianity. It was erroneously believed that the statement in John 1:1 Logos (word) constituted nothing less than a ground-breaking departure from Judaism. However, nothing could be further from the truth. In fact, it is not until verse 14, "and the Word became flesh," that an innovative idea, though not contradictory to Judaism, was first introduced.

The idea of the *Word/Logos/Memrah* of God being the instrument of God in creating the world was not at all new to Second Temple Judaism. For example, Philo, an Alexandrian Jew from the first century, wrote:

> "...the most universal of all things is God; and in the second place the Logos - Word of God." (Allegorical Interpretation, II, 86); "...the shadow of God is His Word - Logos, which He used like an instrument when He was making the world..." (Allegorical Interpretation, III, 96); "This same Word – Logos is continually a suppliant to the immortal God on behalf of the mortal race, which is exposed to affliction and misery; and is also the ambassador, sent by the Ruler of all, to the subject race... neither being uncreated as God, nor yet created as you, but being in the midst between these two

extremities…" ("Who is the Heir of Divine Things," 205-6).

These are only a few examples of this idea. Jesus, as he addresses his followers in Laodicea, is identifying himself with the instrument of God at the creation of the world, the Logos, the word of God (דבר יהוה, *davar yhvh*). This is a thoroughly Jewish idea in the first century. There are also some important things we should know about the city of Laodicea. It is highly likely that Jesus and the human author of the book of Revelation were well aware of these issues. The background always sheds valuable light.

There was more than one city named Laodicea in the ancient world, but this Laodicea of Lycus, located in Asia Minor, was established in approximately 250 BCE by Antiochus of Syria, who named it after his wife, Laodice. Because of its physical location, Laodicea was a wealthy and important city in Asia Minor. The road from Ephesus to the east of Syria was the key road in Asia, and it went through Laodicea. In its path, there was an important detour through which a large portion of trade traffic passed. This fact effectively turned the city into an exclusive provider of goods and services.

Laodicea was originally built as a fortress, even though it had one significant deficiency. All of its water supply had to come by underground aqueduct from springs located at least 3 kilometers (2 miles) away. This was not a good feature for a city when it would be besieged by its enemies. But in Roman times, the city prospered due to the long-lasting peace established and preserved by the Roman Empire.

Several characteristics of the city of Laodicea can be seen through Jesus' address to the congregation located there. First, it was the banking and financial center for Asia Minor. The wealth of the city could be seen in quotations from the Roman historian Tacitus:

> "One of the most famous cities of Asia, Laodicea, was in that same year overthrown by an earthquake and without any relief from us recovered itself by its own resources" (Tacitus, Annals 14: 27).

No wonder Laodicea could boast that it was rich and had amassed wealth and had need of nothing. Second, it was the center of the clothing industry. It mass-produced inexpensive outer wool garments. Third, Laodicea was a medical center of the ancient world. A famous medical school of that tie was located in Laodicea. The names of two of its most famous doctors appear on Laodicean coins. In particular, this medical establishment was famous for producing special medication for ears and eyes.

Last but and not least, Laodicea boasted a disproportionally large Jewish population. In 62 B.C. Flaccus, the governor of the province, became alarmed at the amount of currency the Jews were exporting in payment of the Temple tax that was made by every male Jew. Flaccus imposed an embargo on the export of currency. There were at least 7,000 male Jews residing in the relatively small city. There can have been few areas where the Jews were wealthier and more influential. Yet excessive wealth could be an obstacle to the path of the kingdom.

'I know your deeds, that you are neither cold nor hot; I wish that you were cold or hot. 16 So because you are lukewarm, and neither hot nor cold, I will spit you out of My mouth. (Rev 3:15-16)

The city of Laodicea was located between the cities of Hierapolis and Colossae. Both of these cities were known for the pure waters that flowed through them. Hierapolis had a hot spring that was considered to be medicinal. Colossae was known for its cold, refreshing mountain springs. Laodicea, on the other hand, had a bad reputation when it came to water. With all of their resources, they did not have what their neighbors had. In light of this, we can see that both "hot" and "cold" were considered to be good, while the dirty lukewarm water of Laodicea was of no particular benefit.

Because you say, "I am rich, and have become wealthy, and have need of nothing," and you do not know that you are wretched and miserable and poor and blind and naked, I advise you to buy from Me gold refined by fire so that you may become rich, and white garments so that you may clothe yourself, and that the shame of your nakedness will not be revealed; and eye salve to anoint your eyes so that you may see. Those whom I love, I reprove and discipline; therefore be zealous and repent. (Rev 3: 17-19)

A careful reading of Jesus' admonition reveals that this assembly had become focused on riches and wealth, with pride and spiritual complacency being the result. Jesus called this assembly of his followers to faith and repentance. They had sold out to this world and were so sure of themselves because they did not realize their true state. They were not rich; they were poor. They were not well-dressed, but naked. They were not self-sufficient, but they were truly needy. They thought they had access to one of the best health centers in the Roman Empire, but, they were completely blind. They had invested their valuables in the wrong bank.

What is important to realize is that this letter is no different from the six letters to the other assemblies. The challenge for us is to see that the kind of wealth and comfort mentioned here could have only been achieved if their full participation in pagan Roman society is presumed. Jesus' reproof is not to be taken as heartless, harsh treatment. It is precisely because these people had Christ's redemptive love and commitment that they were challenged to repent and change their ways.

Behold, I stand at the door and knock; if anyone hears My voice and opens the door, I will come in to him and will dine with him, and he with Me. (Rev 3:20)

Israel's King is willing to have real table fellowship with his followers. However, because he is holy, no compromise or contamination with defilement is allowed. This is clearly stated in the Israelite Scriptures. We read in Leviticus 18:24 "Do not defile yourselves by any of these things; for by all these the nations which I am casting out before you have become defiled." The Nicolaitans of Pergamum and Ephesus – those who claimed "we will eat" practiced indiscriminate eating and most likely participated in unrestricted fellowship with Roman paganism. Such a way of life was forbidden by the Jerusalem council in Acts chapter 15.

Many Laodicean followers of the Jewish Christ might have fallen prey to Nicolaitan teachings. Although they are not explicitly identified with them as were others. Jesus, by calling them to repentance, offered them the greatest possible incentive – table fellowship with him.. Anyone who enters into fellowship with Israel's God must remain pure. Nothing has changed since the day God called out to Morse on Sinai. The Holy is still holy.

He who overcomes, I will grant to him to sit down with Me on My throne, as I also overcame and sat down with My Father on His throne. He who has an ear, let him hear what the Spirit says to the assemblies.'" (Rev 3:21-22)

There is no doubt that the commitment to refrain from the defilement of the lifestyle prevalent in the Roman Empire was extremely difficult, especially when non-Jews. Full uniting with the people of Israel (conversion) for those gentiles who followed Jesus was severally discouraged and culturally unacceptable in the Roman Empire. Those who chose to convert were switching their allegiances and were looked upon as untrustworthy, disloyal subjects of the empire, bad citizens.

We read in 1 Cor. 7:17: "Only, as the Lord has assigned to each one, as God has called each, in this manner let him walk. And so, I direct in all the churches." Paul also taught his disciples to maintain their ethnic identities as they were before they decided to follow Jesus. Gentile followers of the Jewish Christ were encouraged to join the Jewish coalition as sojourners with Israel; that is, not as Jews, but as the Nations alongside Israel. And this matches the vision of the prophets of Israel.

In so doing, according to Paul, they would take part in what he called "establishing the Torah." Paul supported the declaration, made at the Jerusalem council, for both Jews and the Nations to worship the LORD God on equal footing and remain as they are. We read what Apostle Paul, the only Pharisee whose writings to the non-Jewish followers of Jesus survive, says about this in Romans:

> For we maintain that a man is justified by faith apart from works of the Torah. Or is God the God of Jews only? Is He not the God of Gentiles also? Yes, of Gentiles also, since indeed God who will justify the circumcised by faith and the uncircumcised through faith is one. Do we then nullify the Torah through faith? May it never be! On the contrary, we establish the Torah. (Romans 3:28-31)

This means that for gentile followers of Jesus, there were not many options. They could either join Jewish people through proselyte conversion (which was culturally taboo) or they could conform to the rules and practices of pagan Rome. A third, and the most difficult, option was to learn how to live holy and righteous lives as the nations in the Roman world while worshiping the same God as Jews but through Jesus - his anointed King. This was not an easy and very new development. In fact, it was extraordinarily difficult because it placed people in the margins. Therefore, the rewards offered are so incredibly great.

Chapter 6: God's Throne

After these things I looked, and behold, a door
standing open in heaven, and the first voice which
I had heard, like the sound of a trumpet speaking
with me, said, "Come up here, and I will show you
what must take place after these things."
Immediately I was in the Spirit; and behold, a
throne was standing in heaven, and One sitting on
the throne. (Rev 4:1-2)

With its open door and call to ascend, this vision is
reminiscent of the dream of Jacob, the patriarch of
Israel. "And behold, a ladder [or, a stairway] set up [and
reaching to] the earth (סֻלָּם מֻצָּב אַרְצָה). And its head
reached to the sky (וְרֹאשׁוֹ מַגִּיעַ הַשָּׁמָיְמָה). And behold,
angels of God (מַלְאֲכֵי אֱלֹהִים) were ascending and
descending on it." (Gen. 28:12) Both Jacob and John
saw some kind of passageway to the heavenly realm.

Moreover, in both Jacob's dream and John's vision, the
viewer appears to be a passive observer. The notion of
being "in the Spirit" seems to emphasize the idea that
an external force initiated the event and John can
observe and interact, but he is not in full control.

In biblical history, monumentally significant events can
occur at times of such human passivity. Adam fell into
a deep sleep so that God could create a wife for him
(Gen. 2:21). Abraham was overcome by the same deep

sleep (טרדמה, *tardemah*) while God spoke to him in the context of "cutting" a new covenant (Gen. 15:12). Such events seem to indicate an active concern for earthly beings on the part of heaven, as opposed to abandoning humanity to its own resources.

Although John's Revelation falls into a literary category called Jewish apocalyptic literature, there are a number of distinctive features that set it apart from other Jewish texts of this variety. In Revelation, John gets immediate and unmediated access to the throne room of God, something that does not usually occur in other Jewish apocalyptic works.

There is a general consensus that John's Revelation displays significant literary dependence on another Jewish apocalyptic text, namely the book of Ezekiel. As an interesting side note, in Eli's earlier book "The Jewish Gospel of John," he argues that whoever wrote John's Gospel was very interested in the book of Ezekiel. The amount of literal and thematic parallels is too great to deny such a connection.

The Book of Revelation was authored by someone named John, a very common Jewish name – (יוחנן, *Yochanan*) which means "God's grace" This John also shows an obvious interest in the book of Ezekiel. It was very common to name apocalyptic Jewish works by the name of some great biblical character (for example, Apocalypse of Elijah, Apocalypse of Daniel, Apocalypse of Moses, and the list can go on and on). What is unusual here is that this apocalypse is attributed to someone named Yohanan (John) who seemingly was without any prior notoriety, except if indeed John the Apostle is the author

Although the evidence is certainly inconclusive (and John's Gospel does a very good job of remaining anonymous), there is an occasional hint to the author in these texts, but only a hint. It t may have been John, Son of Zebedee, who authored it. There are some very good arguments that show the author belonged to a priestly lineage. If it was so, then the author's preoccupation with the book of Ezekiel makes a lot of sense.

One of the major arguments, however, against the Gospel of John and the book of Revelation being written by the same person (no such problem exists between Gospel of John and John's letters) is that the Greek of John's Gospel and that of Revelation is dramatically different. To put it another way, the Greek of John's Gospel is clearly better than that of the Greek of Revelation. But given that most literature was not actually written by its author but dictated through a scribe, the difference in the level of linguistic sophistication could be accounted for by a different scribe doing the work. Another issue is the genre adaptation from a historical narrative (Gospel of John) to an apocalypse (book of Revelation). In other words, if John wrote his Gospel from Ephesus (as some early traditions indicate) it would make sense that he would have had access to some of the best scribes; whereas, while he was on the Island of Patmos, even though it was not technically a prison, it is reasonable to assume that his choice of scribes would have been severally limited, if available at all. Professional scribes were used widely in the production of all sorts of documents, sacred and secular.

And He who was sitting was like a jasper stone and a sardius in appearance; and there was a rainbow around the throne, like an emerald in appearance. (Rev 4:3)

As we begin considering the vision that John recorded for the benefit of others who would read his apocalypse, we must address the text that parallels this one. We will encounter a truly intriguing description in Ezekiel:

> Now above the expanse that was over their heads there was something resembling a throne, like lapis lazuli in appearance, and on that which resembled a throne, high up, was a figure with the appearance of a man. Then I noticed from the appearance of His loins and upward something like glowing metal that looked like fire all around within it, and from the appearance of His loins and downward I saw something like fire, and there was a radiance around Him. As the appearance of the rainbow in the clouds on a rainy day, so was the appearance of the surrounding radiance. Such was the appearance of the likeness of the glory of the Lord. And when I saw it, I fell on my face and heard a voice speaking. (Ezekiel 1:26-27)

The parallels are close and intriguing. What is striking is that they do not give an impression of literal dependence - meaning that John read what Ezekiel wrote and wrote his own material somewhat differently.

Instead, the level of perception of what they saw, and the language is so different (although it is clear they are describing something extremely similar) that the impression the (religious) reader gets is that the same type of vision may have been experienced by both Ezekiel and the author of Revelation.

Around the throne were twenty-four thrones; and upon the thrones I saw twenty-four elders sitting, clothed in white garments, and golden crowns on their heads. (Rev 4:4)

The throne of God is surrounded by another twenty-four thrones with the elders crowned (crowns represent legitimacy) and dressed in white (white garments represent absolute purity and holiness). This feature is unparalleled in any other Jewish apocalyptic work. There are no other visions like this one. The big question, however, is not really the meaning of the crowns and the garments, but the number of the elders. Who are the 24 persons making up God's heavenly council? In Revelation 11:15-19, the 24 elders seem to function as God's chief worshipers with the powers of the mediating priests:

> Then the seventh angel sounded; and there were loud voices in heaven, saying, "The kingdom of the world has become the kingdom of our Lord and of His Christ; and He will reign forever and ever." And the twenty-four elders, who sit on their thrones before God, fell on their faces and worshiped God, saying, "We give You thanks, O Lord God, the Almighty, who are and who were, because You have taken Your great power and have begun

to reign. And the nations were enraged, and
Your wrath came, and the time came for the
dead to be judged, and the time to reward Your
bond-servants the prophets and the saints and
those who fear Your name, the small and the
great, and to destroy those who destroy the
earth." And the temple of God which is in
heaven was opened; and the ark of His
covenant appeared in His temple, and there
were flashes of lightning and sounds and peals
of thunder and an earthquake and a great
hailstorm. (Rev. 11:15-19)

Another relevant text that shows the 24 elders in action
is found in Revelation 19:3-5. There we read that the 24
elders were a very important part of the polyphony of
heavenly voices, whether they were priestly or not clear:

And a second time they said, "Hallelujah! Her
smoke rises up forever and ever." And the
twenty-four elders and the four living creatures
fell down and worshiped God who sits on the
throne saying, "Amen. Hallelujah! (Revelation
19:3-4.)

While this assertion is not certain, the best possible
candidate for the 24 elders around God's throne is the
unity government of the original and the now renewed
Israel, i.e., twelve heads of the tribes of Israel plus
twelve additional heads of Israel – the apostles of Jesus.
This is speculative of course, because the texts do not
tell us. Whether the beginning of the night visions of
Daniel in chapter 7 can shed any light on the heavenly
courtroom throne (vs. 9) motif is not clear, since we do
not know if the 24 thrones (the elders) are in view or

only two (the Ancient of Days and the Son of Man).
We read in Daniel:

> "I kept looking until thrones were set up, and
> the Ancient of Days took His seat; His vesture
> was like white snow and the hair of His head
> like pure wool. His throne was ablaze with
> flames, its wheels were a burning fire." (Daniel
> 7:9)

Since Daniel 7:13-14 describes the crowning ceremony
of the Son of Man, it stands to reason to assume that
the plurality of the thrones in Daniel 7:9 refers to two
thrones only:

> "I kept looking in the night visions, and
> behold, with the clouds of heaven One like a
> Son of Man was coming, and He came up to
> the Ancient of Days. And was presented before
> Him. "And to Him was given dominion, Glory
> and a kingdom, that all the peoples, nations
> and men of every language might serve Him.
> His dominion is an everlasting dominion,
> which will not pass away. And His kingdom is
> one which will not be destroyed." (Daniel 7:13-
> 14)

There is a caveat that deserves a note here. Modern
translations translate the twenty-four thrones as we are
accustomed to reading - "twenty-four," but the Greek
manuscripts preserve the ancient Hebraic reversed
numbering "four and twenty." The meaning is the
same, but the Hebraism is preserved only in some more
archaic translations

Out from the throne come flashes of lightning and sounds and peals of thunder. And there were seven lamps of fire burning before the throne, which are the seven Spirits of God; and before the throne there was something like a sea of glass, like crystal; (Rev 4:5-6)

This text is extremely close to the description given in Ezekiel 1:26-27 quoted above. The heavenly menorah (the seven lamps of fire) is shown to be a symbol of the seven Spirits of God (see the earlier discussion on John 1:4 where the Spirits are first mentioned). The glory of the Ancient of Days is here described in terms of the magnificence of the heavenly throne and the heavenly throne room, if we can speak of it in such a way, since God's throne is not situated it seems in one particular place but is essentially a traveling throne-chariot (מֶרְכָּבָה, *merkavah*) for Israel's God. in Jewish studies This area of discussion is usually referred to as Merkavah Mysticism – the experience of seeing the heavenly, in this case, the traveling throne of the יהוה (LORD) God himself.

"And in the center and around the throne, four living creatures full of eyes in front and behind. The first creature was like a lion, and the second creature like a calf, and the third creature had a face like that of a man, and the fourth creature was like a flying eagle. And the four living creatures, each one of them having six wings, are full of eyes around and within; and day and night they do not cease to say, 'Holy, holy, holy is the Lord God, the Almighty, who was and who is and who is to come.'" (Rev 4:6-8)

This passage gives an impression of both Ezekiel's and Isaiah's visions expanded. The living beings of Ezekiel 1-11 are identified with the six-winged creatures of Isaiah 6. In fact, these descriptions of God's four special servants are merged in the prophetic vision of John in this text. There are some variations in the very last section of the vision, however. Consider what Isaiah saw:

> Seraphim stood above Him, each having six wings: with two he covered his face, and with two he covered his feet, and with two he flew. And one called out to another and said, 'Holy, Holy, Holy, is the Lord of hosts, The whole earth is full of His glory.' (Isaiah 6:2-3)

And now look at the words of Ezekiel:

> Now over the heads of the living beings there was something like an expanse, like the awesome gleam of crystal, spread out over their heads. Under the expanse their wings were stretched out straight, one toward the other; each one also had two wings covering its body on the one side and on the other. (Ezekiel 1:22-23)

Both in Ezekiel and in Revelation, the four living beings are situated under the traveling throne-chariot of God, forming a squire as it were through the wings that all touch each other's wings and the wheels that always move together with the living beings. The expanse separates them (the bottom of the heavenly chariot throne) from the glorious God himself (יהוה, *yhvh*) sitting on his throne that is situated directly over them from the opposite side.

The emphasis on the eyes of these beings speaks clearly of their ability to see and track all events in the created order simultaneously. Their eyes do not look in one direction alone but in all possible directions. God himself, of course, sees everything and knows all things. A body has always been considered the symbol of creatureliness. Therefore, their nature as having been created had to be covered with wings to show the true honor that is rendered by these magnificent beings to the uncreated God.

The joyful praise of God is a well-attested theme in a wide variety of Jewish literature. For example, in the Qumran scrolls, which predate Revelation by a century, we see this curious description:

> Praise the God of the lofty heights, O your
> lofty ones among all the gods of knowledge.
> Let the holiest of the godlike ones sanctify the
> King of glory who sanctifies by holiness all His
> holy ones. O you chiefs of the praises of all the
> godlike beings, praise the splendidly
> praiseworthy God. For in the splendor of
> praise is the glory of His realm... Sing with joy,
> you who rejoice in His knowledge with
> rejoicing among the wondrous godlike beings.
> And chant His glory with the tongue of all who
> chant with knowledge; and chant His
> wonderful songs of joy with the mouth of all
> who chant of Him. For He is God of all who
> rejoices forever and Judge in His power of all
> the spirits of understanding. (The Song of
> Sabbath Sacrifice, 4Q403).

The idea of God being surrounded by many godlike heavenly angelic beings is something many writers note. And this liturgical Qumran texts testify of heavenly praise.

"And when the living creatures give glory and honor and thanks to Him who sits on the throne, to Him who lives forever and ever, the twenty-four elders will fall down before Him who sits on the throne, and will worship Him who lives forever and ever, and will cast their crowns before the throne, saying, 'Worthy are You, our Lord and our God, to receive glory and honor and power; for You created all things, and because of Your will they existed and were created.'" (Rev 4:9-11)

John was allowed to witness not only the structure of the heavenly traveling throne-chariot of God but also the actual liturgy – the order of worship that takes place in heaven wherever God is worshiped. In vs. 9-11 the order is stated as follows: First, the four living creatures give glory, honor, and thanks to the one sitting on the throne, then the twenty-four elders prostrate themselves before him, casting down their own crowns. The content of their confession is specified in terms of God's worthiness, honor, and power and is rooted in the act of creation.

I saw in the right hand of Him who sat on the throne a book written inside and on the back, sealed up with seven seals. (Rev 5:1)

Once Jesus had addressed the seven assemblies in Asia Minor and presented the hearers of his message a glimpse into the heavenly throne room Revelation switches to yet another vision. John saw that the one who was seated on the throne holding a scroll on his hand. The text literally says "on" and not "in" And this scroll had writing on the front and the back.

If we imagine something that resembles a Torah scroll used in Jewish worship today, we would not be far from something John describes. A scroll (מְגִילָה, *megillah*) would not always have two rollers as books used for liturgical reading in the synagogues. Consider shorter scrolls, such as Esther; they typically have only one roller. Plus, scrolls like these are usually written on one side, and the other side is blank. The scroll in this vision is written on both sides. And this was common in the ancient world. Writing materials were very expensive. Sometimes both sides were fully used for pragmatic reasons. It is possible that Ezek.1-2 is describing such a scroll.

Sometimes the outside writing merely summed up what was inside, especially if the scroll was not very long and if it was secured by seals. This scroll was secured by seven seals. This would safeguard what was written inside. Both the outside writing and the seals would prevent anyone unqualified from unrolling it.

The idea of sealing an important document was also not unusual. This was a common practice. Nor is the number of the seals entirely unique. John draws on the symbolism of seven continuously. The seals were not designed to conceal the content inside; but rather to protect it from any alterations. The seals are not that easy to break accidentally. But if they are broken, there is no way to know if the contents were not somehow altered. In fact, the seals testified that the words inside were genuine, sealed by the one who authored them. This concern was valid and can be seen in the end of Revelation. The scribes and anyone else was explicitly warned about adding or deleting anything from John's writings:

> I testify to everyone who hears the words of the prophecy of this book: if anyone adds to them, God will add to him the plagues which are written in this book; and if anyone takes away from the words of the book of this prophecy, God will take away his part from the tree of life and from the holy city, which are written in this book. (Revelation 22:18-19)

It is not clear why he who sat on the throne (and we are not told who it was) could not open the scroll himself. Why did he someone else to do it? Whatever the reason, it is likely that we are witnessing the heavenly court ceremony that is either identical to or connected with Daniel 7:

> "I kept looking in the night visions, and behold, with the clouds of heaven One like a Son of Man was coming, and He came up to the Ancient of Days and was presented before Him. "And to Him was given dominion, Glory and a kingdom that all the peoples, nations and men of every language might serve Him. His dominion is an everlasting dominion which will not pass away; and His kingdom is one which will not be destroyed." (Daniel 7:13-14)

Perhaps the scroll in Rev. 5:1 had some kind of connection to the scroll described in the book of Ezekiel. In fact, this vision could be completely original to John but reads a little like an adaptation of both Dan. 7:13-14 and Ezek. 2:8-10.

> Now you, son of man, listen to what I am speaking to you; do not be rebellious like that rebellious house. Open your mouth and eat what I am giving you." Then I looked, and behold, a hand was extended to me, and lo, a scroll was in it. When He spread it out before me, it was written on the front and back, and written on it were lamentations, mourning, and woe. (Ezekiel 2:8-10)

It is also possible that Isaiah 29 may have been the text that inspired John to write what he did:

> "The entire vision will be to you like the words of a sealed book, which when they give it to the one who is literate, saying, 'Please read this,' he will say, 'I cannot, for it is sealed.'" (Isaiah 29:11)

In chapter 3 of Ezekiel, God tells the author to eat the entire scroll as he prepares for his prophetic ministry that will likely not be received by the rebellious house of Israel. This is a bizarre and unusual picture. The house of Israel in Ezekiel should not be confused with the entire people of Israel but understood as only the Northern Kingdom. In Ezekiel, the southern Kingdom is referred to as the house of Judah. This is a common dynamic present in many of Israel's prophets. Though Judah is also Israel, the kingdom is treated separately.

There are both similarities and differences here. One similarity is that the scroll was offered by God and that it was written on both the inner and the outer sides. The difference was that it was unrolled. Presumably, the prophet could see what was written before he ate it. The scroll offered to Ezekiel was about lamentation, mourning and woe. The scroll in Revelation 5:1 may be a very similar scroll. It, if was then what was written inside, may have been ominous as well

Moreover, the idea of a book of heavenly records has deep roots in Hebrew and Jewish scriptural traditions. For example, Psalm 139:6 says, "Your eyes have seen my unformed substance; And in Your book were all written the days that were ordained for me, when as yet there was not one of them." Or in Exodus 32:32, where we read: "But now, if You will, forgive their sin - and if not, please blot me out from Your book which You have written!" We have already encountered this terminology in Revelation 3:5 "He who overcomes will thus be clothed in white garments; and I will not erase his name from the book of life, and I will confess his name before My Father and before His angels."

This book, however, appears to be different. We will no doubt discover much more about the nature of the content and function of this book in this passage as it unfolds. Unlike many surrounding nations, Jewish culture was a very literate culture and images of books, scrolls, records of all sorts, writing, and reading are common. The main part of synagogue worship was dependent on the public reading from the scroll and teachings that explained what was being read.

And I saw a mighty angel proclaiming with a loud voice, "Who is worthy to open the book and to break its seals?" And no one in heaven or on the earth or under the earth was able to open the book or to look into it. (Rev 5:2-3)

John saw an angel who was called a "mighty angel" (ἄγγελον ἰσχυρὸν, *angelon ischuron*). This could be a reference to a high-ranking angel in terms of the heavenly hierarchy. It may be one of the angels known to us by name, but visually unknown to John the Seer. It was this angel, that was given the sacred task of announcing the great message. He did so in a loud voice – the basic idea is that this message would be heard by everyone. No one, on or under the face of the earth could say that they did not hear the call for the one who is worthy. No stone was left unturned. No one was found.

This drama of looking for someone who is worthy is for the benefit of the listeners of John's message. They probably know who is worthy, but the drama plays out further.

Then I began to weep greatly because no one was found worthy to open the book or to look into it; (Rev 5:4)

It is very interesting that John saw himself in the vision. He was not simply reacting to what he saw, but he saw himself reacting, playing a part of this heavenly dramatic moment. He, too, was a part of this great heavenly scene. When we read the words of verses 1-3 we are not moved to tears, and we do not break into uncontrolled weeping as if we had lost all hope.

Why did John weep? Many modern readers of Revelation do not have such a strong reaction to these words. Yet, in the context of the vision, the very fate of the entire universe apparently hinges on finding someone who is worthy to unseal the scroll. Moreover, John was experiencing sensations and emotions corresponding to the heavenly reality rather than normal earthly (human) perception. Why couldn't the One sitting on the throne open the scroll himself? We are not told, but the opening of the scroll seems to represent a ceremony of the heavenly court.

The scene is connected to Biblical visions recorded by Daniel and Ezekiel. In Daniel 7:13-14, "one like a son of man" comes to the Ancient of Days and receives power, dominion, and glory. In Ezekiel 2:8-10, " a son of man" is told to eat a scroll "inscribed on the inside and on the back with lamentations, mourning, and woe."

> And you, son of man, hear what I say unto you! Do not be rebellious like that rebellious house. Open your mouth and eat what I give you. And I saw, and behold, a hand sent out to me; and behold, a scroll of a book in it. And he spread it before me; and it was inscribed on the inside and on the back, inscribed with lamentations, mourning, and woe. (Ezek. 2:8-10)

In addition to Dan. 7:13-14 and Ezek. 2:8-10, John's vision may draw from other Hebrew prophecies as well. Such allusions and literary connections would have been familiar to his audience – even expected.

> And [this] entire vision will be to you as the words of a sealed book, which [people] give to one who is learned, saying: Please read this; but he says: I cannot! for it is sealed. (Isa. 29:11)

Yochanan was in heaven when this happened. He was able to experience the moment on a wholly different level. He cried bitterly.

and one of the elders said to me, "Stop weeping; behold, the Lion that is from the tribe of Judah, the Root of David... (Rev 5:5a)

Normally in Jewish apocalyptic visions, the seer asks questions of the revealer (typically an angel), but in Revelation, this usual technique is absent. Anything that John needed to know was being shown and told to him by others without any requests. One of the elders who seemed to function as a special spokesman for the twenty-four elders seated on the thrones (Dan.7:9; Rev. 4:4) announced a word of hope to John. He should look towards someone who had escaped his attention – someone who within himself combined qualities that are worthy of the royal epithet "the Lion of the Tribe of Judah" (Gen.49:9) and "the Root of David" (Is.11:1, 10). Consider these relevant passages for a deeper understanding of this unique title:

> "Judah, your brothers shall praise you; your hand shall be on the neck of your enemies;

your father's sons shall bow down to you.
Judah is a lion's whelp; from the prey, my son,
you have gone up. He couches, he lies down as
a lion, and as a lion, who dares rouse him up?
The scepter shall not depart from Judah, nor
the ruler's staff from between his feet, until
Shiloh comes, and to him shall be the
obedience of the peoples." (Genesis 49:8-10)

Why Lion of Judah? Reuben was the firstborn of
Jacob's twelve sons, yet it was Judah who would be
recognized as the leader and ruler of his brothers.
Jacob's prophetic blessing compares Judah to a lion and
speaks of his rulership. Jacob says יִשְׁתַּחֲווּ לְךָ בְּנֵי אָבִיךְ
(*yishtachavu lekha benei avikha*) "your father's sons shall
bow to you." The שֵׁבֶט (*shevet*) "scepter," a sign of
tribal/princely authority, shall not depart from him; the
מְחֹקֵק (*mechoqeq*) "legislator's staff" will always be planted
firmly between his feet.

How and why did Judah become preeminent among his
brothers instead of the firstborn, Reuben?

When the brothers plotted to murder Joseph, it was
Reuben who convinced them not to kill him. He
suggested throwing him into a pit and planned to rescue
his brother later (Gen. 37:22). Judah then proposed a
more "profitable" route of selling their brother as a
slave (Gen. 37:26). And indeed, Joseph became a slave.

Joseph rose to power in Egypt. Upon seeing his
brothers so many years later, he concealed his identity
and wove a complex intrigue to test them. He accursed
his brothers of being spies and demanded they bring
Benjamin to Egypt. Joseph framed Benjamin for a

crime that would carry dreadful punishment and observed the response of his brothers.

Benjamin appeared to be guilty; they tore their clothes and mourned the inevitable loss. Initially, Jacob refused to allow Benjamin to go to Egypt because he feared losing him. Judah convinced him by assuming personal responsibility for Benjamin. Now in Egypt, Judah had a choice to abandon Benjamin as he did Joseph many years earlier or try to save him.

Throughout the incident, the brothers felt the guilt of their earlier crime and surmised that their current predicament is a punishment for that betrayal. This time Judah offered his own life in exchange for Benjamin (Gen. 44:30-34). And this is when Joseph broke down and wept before his brothers. He revealed who he really was and that he had forgiven them.

Despite his sins and weaknesses, Judah rather than Reuben emerged as a true leader among his brothers. The key moment in the story is when Judah becomes willing to die (or become a slave forever) to sacrifice himself.

Judah is compared to a lion and promised the rule of Israel. The royal line of Israel's kings would come from Judah. The descent from both Judah and David was a necessary qualification of the Messiah. The accounts of the life of Jesus accordingly stress his heritage to this very family line.

> Then a shoot will spring from the stem of
> Jesse, and a branch from his roots will bear

fruit. The Spirit of the Lord will rest on Him…
and He will delight in the fear of the Lord, and
He will not judge by what His eyes see, nor
make a decision by what His ears hear; but
with righteousness He will judge the poor, and
decide with fairness for the afflicted of the
earth; and He will strike the earth with the rod
of His mouth, and with the breath of His lips
He will slay the wicked… Then in that day the
nations will resort to the root of Jesse, who will
stand as a signal for the peoples; and his resting
place will be glorious. (Isaiah 11:1-10)

Both the Genesis and Isaiah texts here (Revelation 5)
form one picture of Christ Jesus as the descendent both
of Judah and David, who is fully qualified to rule Israel
and the nations, because he has shown himself to be
victorious and prevail over all the enemies, both his
own and God's.

"…has overcome so as to open the book and its seven seals." (Rev 5:5b)

It is important to note that the worthiness of the one
who could break the seals and open the book was not
based on his person. In other words, he was defined as
the one who overcame, which is an act or a deed This
idea of overcoming comes up repeatedly, not only in
the message of Revelation itself (Rev.2-3) but also in
the letters of John (1 John 2:13-14, 5:4-5). It is also
present in John 16:33, "These things I have spoken to
you, so that in Me you may have peace. In the world,
you have tribulation but take courage; I have overcome
the world."

Two points of evidence keep moving us towards a position that the same person wrote all books traditionally attributed to John: 1) the importance of Daniel and Ezekiel for both the Gospel of John and Revelation (see the Jewish Gospel of John book) and 2) the idea of "overcoming". While it is not a strong motif in John's gospel, it is a very strong theme in John's letters. This by itself is a serious argument. If a solid connection between John's letters and Revelation can be established, then the connection between Revelation and John's gospel should also not be rejected since there are few doubts that John's Gospel and his letters were authored by one and the same person.

And I saw between the throne (with the four living creatures) and the elders a Lamb standing, as if slain, having seven horns and seven eyes, which are the seven Spirits of God, sent out into all the earth. (Rev 5:6)

The Greek phrase "between the throne" (ἐν μέσῳ τοῦ θρόνου) in this verse should be more accurately translated as "in the midst of the throne" or even "in the center of the throne." There is no problem at all here with the symbol of Jesus (slain lamb) being found on God's throne. Similar ideas could be found in the Jewish thinking of that time regarding the throne of God. For example, in 1 Enoch 69, we have one such Jewish speculation concerning the concept of Daniel's Son of Man vision and how that should be understood:

> ...and from henceforth there shall be nothing
> corruptible; for that Son of Man has appeared
> and has seated himself on the throne of his

> glory, and all evil shall pass away before his
> face, and the word of that Son of Man shall go
> forth and be strong before the Lord of Spirits.
> (1 Enoch 69)

In this quotation, we see an idea that is very similar to the Son of Man sitting on the throne of God's glory. Given the basic idea that only gods get to sit in heaven (all others do not sit but stand in worship) the one who sits has divine status. This is a very important observation that places the book of Revelation under the wide umbrella of first-century Israelite thought on this topic. Of course, there is no way to be certain, and the range of possible meanings, including "between the throne" and other thrones set up nearby (those of the elders) should also be considered. But this scenario is equally possible.

And He came and took the book out of the right hand of Him who sat on the throne. When He had taken the book, the four living creatures and the twenty-four elders fell down before the Lamb, each one holding a harp and golden bowls full of incense, which are the prayers of the saints. (Rev 5:7-8)

To us it is clear that these verses reflect a widespread Jewish idea of the duality of God. Not all Jews embraced this, but a Jewish *Logos/Memrah* theology is in view here. When the Lamb came and took the book from the hand of the One who sat upon the main throne, the elders and four heavenly figures fell down or worshiped before the Lamb. The act of falling down symbolized not only their own worship but also the worship of those they represented – the righteous people of Israel and the nations and their heartfelt prayers.

In keeping with the Gospel of John, the book of Revelation sets forth what some scholars call "high-Christology", showing Jesus as God, and not as half God or somewhat God. However, in keeping with both John's gospel and the previously cited Enoch material, the distinction between the LORD God and the Jewish Logos (Son of Man/Lamb) is also upheld - the Son is submissive to the Father. Later Christian theologians called this "subordination" Moreover, the Son, while being (using theological language) "equal in power and glory" to the Father, is not the Father. He, being his son, is distinct from him. Yet, in a customary Jewish way, this is not all spelled out plainly. The recipients of the message must connect the dots themselves, and faith is required to come to a conclusion and understanding of how the Father and Son are connected.

The idea of a lamb or ram is also traditional. The seer of 1 Enoch recorded a dream based on the history of Israel (ch. 85-90). In this dream, all people were represented by animals. Great kings of Israel are portrayed as rams. The nation's leaders are also termed "shepherds of the sheep," while God is called the "Lord of the sheep" (cf.: Ezek. 34:31; Psa. 79:13, 95:7, 100:3).

> And I [still] saw until a throne was erected in the pleasant land, and the Lord of the sheep sat down upon it, and the other one took the sealed scrolls and opened those scrolls before the Lord of the sheep. (1 Enoch 90:20)

It would be hard to miss the similarities between this vision and John's story in Revelation. In fact, more connections can be seen.

> And I saw that a white bull with large horns was born... And I [still] saw until all their generations were transformed, and they all became white bulls; and the first among them became a lamb, and that lamb became a great animal and had great black horns on its head; and the Lord of the sheep rejoiced over it and over all the oxen. And I slept in their midst: and I awoke and saw everything. This is the vision which I saw while I slept...(1 Enoch 90:37-40)

We observe the elders, in their role as priestly staff, mediating the prayers and worship of the righteous, participating equipped with harps and golden bowls of incense. The beautiful polyphonic heavenly liturgy is described in wonderful and truly inspiring detail, beginning with vs. 8 and concluding with vs. 14. As we move through the verses, note how the number of praising and worshiping individuals grows exponentially. It begins with the four living creatures and the twenty-four elders falling down in worship before the Lamb of God.

And they sang a new song, saying, "Worthy are You to take the book and to break its seals; for You were slain, and purchased for God with Your blood men from every tribe and tongue and people and nation. "You have made them to be a kingdom

***and priests to our God; and they will reign upon
the earth." (Rev 5:9-10)***

Even though the elders took part in the priestly
activities of offering the people's prayers before God
and the Lamb in golden bowls, this beautiful worship
of the elders and the four creatures highlights the
priestly/sacrificial functions of Christ Jesus himself. In
John's gospel, the "Good Shepherd" is the one who
lays his life down for his sheep. Here, in the book of
Revelation, Jesus is praised for this very act –
purchasing the people with his own blood. The
redemption that Jesus brings applies to every tribe,
tongue, people, and every nation. Through this
redemption, they have been mysteriously joined to the
royal priesthood of Israel.

Speaking about Israel in Exodus, Moses announced
God's words, "...and you shall be to Me a kingdom of
priests and a holy nation.' These are the words that you
shall speak to the sons of Israel." (Exodus 19:6) Then
many years later, Peter, when writing to a group of
Israelite followers of Yeshua (Jesus) joined by the
faithful from the nations, retorted: "But you are a
chosen race, a royal priesthood, a holy nation, a people
for God's possession, so that you may proclaim the
excellence of Him who has called you out of darkness
into His marvelous light." (1 Peter 2:9)

If we consider this broad idea the body of priests on
earth has grown and expanded to include non-Jewish
priestly staff from every nation of the world. While the
framework of the Book of Revelation is thoroughly
Jewish, here we witness a theological move from tribal

to universal perspective. This in and of itself must be understood as a theological move within Judaism, however, and not from Judaism to something else. In other words, Israel's God redeeming for himself people from every nation. This is not in contradiction with the concept of Jewish worship. It rather establishes and confirms it an original vision of entire humanity recognizing one true God. "God is not God of the Jews only, he is also the God of the Nations, (Rom.3:29)" as Paul has already argued from within the framework of his Jesus-following Pharisaic Judaism.

This is where Revelation and John's gospel, although not in contradiction, part company in their respective emphases. As Eli explains in his book "The Jewish Gospel of John: Discovering Jesus, King of All Israel", John was written almost exclusively to an inner-Israelite audience. The book of Revelation was originally explicitly addressed to the seven historic assemblies in Asia Minor, where Jews and non-Jews together worshiped God in Christ Jesus. God-fearing non-Jews were probably present in significant numbers in this context. And that is perhaps is reflected in the writer's language. The language changes with the audience.

Then I looked, and I heard the voice of many angels around the throne and the living creatures and the elders; and the number of them was myriads of myriads, and thousands of thousands, saying with a loud voice, (Rev 7:11-12)

Notice that as this heavenly liturgy continues increasing numbers of people and creatures join the worship of the Lamb. Now it is not only the four living creatures and the twenty-four elders but also myriads of myriads and thousands of thousands who join in the liturgy. The content of the liturgy they all were reciting clearly links Jesus to the Son of Man in Daniel 7:14. There can be no further doubt about this. "Worthy is the Lamb that was slain to receive power and riches and wisdom and might and honor and glory and blessing. "Remember that in Daniel?

> I kept looking in the night visions, and behold, with the clouds of heaven One like a Son of Man was coming, and He came up to the Ancient of Days and was presented before Him. 'And to Him was given dominion, glory and a kingdom that all the peoples, nations and men of every language might serve Him. (Daniel in 7:13-14)

Like Judah, and like the "Good Shepherd" of the Book of John, the Lion/Lamb has sacrificed his own life for others – his own people and also those "of every tribe and tongue and nation." He has "purchased them for God with his blood."

The Lamb's action attaches people of all lands to the "priestly kingdom" of Israel (see Exod. 19:6). The Hebrew prophet Isaiah also predicted a day when God would restore Israel, taking priests and Levites from other nations to join those of Israel in serving him.

> [The time] is coming to gather all the nations and the tongues; and they shall come and see my glory... And they shall tell my glory among the nations...And they shall bring all your brothers from all the nations as an offering to

the Lord – on horses, and in chariots, and in litters, and on mules, and on camels – to my holy mountain Jerusalem, says the Lord, even as the sons of Israel bring the [prescribed] offering in a clean vessel to the house of the Lord. And I shall also take [some] of them for priests [and] for Levites,' says the Lord." (Is. 66:18b-21)

Worthy is the slain Lamb to receive power and riches and wisdom and might and honor and glory and blessing! (Rev. 5:12b)

This song to the slain Lamb strongly resembles Daniel's account of the Son of Man: "And to him was given dominion, glory, and a kingdom, so that all the peoples, nations and tongues would serve Him." (Dan. 7:14)

And every created thing which is in heaven and on the earth and under the earth and on the sea, and all things in them, I heard saying "To Him who sits on the throne, and to the Lamb, be blessing and honor and glory and dominion forever and ever." (Rev 7:13b)

Once again, the description of the number of worshipers increases and extends even further. Now it includes all created beings everywhere throughout the earth (people, animals, and birds), under the earth (possible monsters of the abyss and supernatural powers are in view here as well) and even in the sea (fish and any other creature that the ancients could imagine inhabited the uncontrollable sea world). The content of their confession is clear. They praise God.

Again, this joint worship of God and the Lamb is very similar to portrayals of the "Son of Man" in both Daniel and 1 Enoch.

> Yea, before the sun and the signs were created, before the stars of the heaven were made, his name was named before the Lord of Spirits... and he shall be the light of the nation's [or, Gentiles]... All who dwell on earth shall fall down and worship before him, and will praise and bless and celebrate with song the Lord of Spirits... (1 Enoch 48)

Next comes another interesting title:

And the four living creatures kept saying, "Amen." And the elders fell down and worshiped. (Rev 7:14)

As the song and the words sounded, the four living creatures continuously repeated the word that in the Jewish psyche relates to verifiable truth, absolute agreement, and full and complete faith in the statement confirmed by it. This word of course is "Amen" (אָמֵן, *amen*) – one of the best known, if not the best-known Hebrew word in the world.

Earlier in John's letter, the heavenly High Priest himself is called ὁ Ἀμήν (ho Amen) "the Amen" (Rev. 3:14). Revelation thus literally identifies the Lion–Lamb–Messiah with ultimate Truth and Stability. He is described as the "faithful witness" and "beginning of Creation" upon whom rest the existence and fate of the entire universe.

Chapter 7: The Seven Seals

Then I saw when the Lamb broke one of the seven seals, and I heard one of the four living creatures saying as with a voice of thunder, "Come." (Rev 6:1)

The message Revelation was either authored during or in anticipation of persecution of especially, non-Jewish followers of Messiah (Christ) in the Roman Empire. The message of the entire book, among other things, sought to provide a true encouragement for the believers who were suffering for their faith and would soon suffer even more. This passage is incredibly important for this to be accomplished. John describes seeing four horses (as we will see shortly, each one symbolized some kind of coming devastation– conquest, sword, famine, and death). While it important to see what each horse symbolizes, especially in its connections with the prophetic material of the Hebrew Bible, by far the most important thing in this passage is the word "Come!" uttered by the four living beings.

While horrible things will soon come to test all the believers, none of them would happen without God's knowledge and command. In other words, as we will see each time a horse leaves its abode, about to wreak havoc on the earth, it is God's angels (four living beings) that give them the command to commence their mission. They cannot move by themselves. They are under God's complete authority. But this is not surprising. When we refer to the literary background of this text found in the Hebrew Bible, we discover that the four horses/riders are also committed servants of God. They are not evil beings or demons unleashed by God to torture humanity, but in fact, are spirits, or angels of God's heavenly patrol, approved and commissioned by Him. In Zachariah, we read about a similar heavenly patrol on four horses:

> ...the word of the Lord came to Zechariah the prophet, the son of Berechiah, the son of Iddo, as follows: 8 I saw at night, and behold, a man was riding on a red horse, and he was standing among the myrtle trees which were in the ravine, with red, sorrel and white horses behind him. 9 Then I said, 'My lord, what are these?' And the angel who was speaking with me said to me, 'I will show you what these are.' 10 And the man who was standing among the myrtle trees answered and said, 'These are those whom the Lord has sent to patrol the earth.' 11 So they answered the angel of the Lord who was standing among the myrtle trees and said, 'We have patrolled the earth, and behold, all the earth is peaceful and quiet.' (Zachariah 1:7-11)

> Now I lifted up my eyes again and looked, and behold, four chariots were coming forth from between the two mountains; and the mountains were bronze mountains. 2 With the first chariot were red horses, with the second chariot black horses, 3 with the third chariot white horses, and with the fourth chariot strong dappled horses. 4 Then I spoke and said to the angel who was speaking with me, 'What are these, my lord?' 5 The angel replied to me,

> 'These are the four spirits of heaven, going
> forth after standing before the Lord of all the
> earth…' (Zachariah 6:1-5)

Hopefully, you see how knowing the words of
Zechariah helps us to interpret what is happening in
Revelation. The writer draws on culturally familiar
imagery.

**I looked, and behold, a white horse, and he who sat
on it had a bow; and a crown was given to him, and
he went out conquering and to conquer. (Rev 6:2)**

As the four seals are opened, we are told about each
horse. At the opening of the first seal, the white horse
was commanded to come forth. The rider of this horse
brings judgment by conquest. This is symbolized by a
bow which was one of the main symbols of ancient
warfare. He was given a crown that symbolized
successful rule over those he conquered. In the years
past, God brought Israel to repentance more than once
by sending foreign conquerors.

**When He broke the second seal, I heard
the second living creature saying, "Come." And
another, a red horse, went out; and to him who sat
on it, it was granted to take peace from the earth,
and that men would slay one another; and a great
sword was given to him. (Rev 6:3-4)**

As the second seal was broken, a rider on the red horse
came forth. The authority that God gave this rider was
to bring a cessation of peace to the earth, causing war
between its residents between one neighbor and

another. This is not a war with foreign conquerors, this is a civil war. This horse, therefore, symbolizes judgment by the sword. The cessation of peace is portrayed as a universal phenomenon and is probably, a conscious reference to a reversal of the *Pax Romana* established under Augustus.

When the seventh seal is opened in Rev.8:1, the result seems anti-climactic with silence for half an hour. It, therefore, appears that the seven seals, now opened, are but a forerunner of the plagues that are heralded by the sounding of the heavenly trumpet (Rev.8:2-11:18).

When He broke the third seal, I heard the third living creature saying, "Come." I looked, and behold, a black horse; and he who sat on it had a pair of scales in his hand. And I heard something like a voice in the center of the four living creatures saying, "A quart of wheat for a denarius, and three quarts of barley for a denarius; and do not damage the oil and the wine." (Rev 6:5)

As Jesus opened the third seal, John reported that he saw a black horse come forth as commanded. The rider of this horse held measuring scales used for wheat and barley sales in his hand. The judgment brought on the earth by this rider was the judgment of famine. The shortage of food disrupts everything and creates havoc in society. John further reported that he heard a voice coming from the four living creatures that spoke of extraordinarily high market prices for wheat and barley and fear that the supply of oil and wine would be damaged. This sudden exclamation seems to be voiced by God. Based on some calculations, we are talking here about the price for wheat and barley that was eight times higher than the average price in the Roman Empire at that time.

The normal cost for a *choinix* (quart) of wheat was about one-eighth of a Greek denarius, while barley was twice cheaper (2 Kings 7:1, 16; Polybius 2.15.1). The message is unambiguous. Families would be able to survive, but they would only be able to afford the bare minimum necessary for survival (Matt. 2:20; Herodotus 7.187; Cicero, In Verrem 3.81). Yet what we read about here is not the sharpest price hike known in history. The prices mentioned in Xenophon Anabasis 1.5.5-6 are 50 times the normal rates. Hence, we should draw a conclusion. This would be a bad time, but not as terrible as humans have endured before. No money will be left for other things, like wine and oil, just enough for bread. That would be difficult but possible to live without in the context of Israelite society

Conquering armies did not always destroy gardens (olive groves and grapevines) because often, the conquered people would pay tribute from the food they produced. But when the goal of a military campaign was to wreak absolute havoc and devastation (punishment), significantly reducing the possibility of sustained existence, food sources were destroyed as well. According to Josephus, Titus, for example, destroyed agricultural complexes around Jerusalem in 66-70 C.E.[14]

---

[14] Josephus, Wars 6.7.

The measure of a quart of wheat and three quarts of barley seem to correspond to one daily needs for a man (Herodotus 7.187) and a horse (Polybius 6.39.13). This, of course, makes sense because the statement is issued directly to the horse rider. A variety of Jewish traditions speak of significant inflation and price increases connected with the arrival of the Messiah. For example, wine will be available, but it will be costly (Babylonian Talmud, Sota 49b). The final wicked generation before the coming of the Messiah will produce no oil or wine (Jubilees 23:18).

When the Lamb broke the fourth seal, I heard the voice of the fourth living creature saying, "Come." I looked, and behold, an ashen horse; and he who sat on it had the name Death; and Hades was following with him. Authority was given to them over a fourth of the earth, to kill with sword and with famine and with pestilence and by the wild beasts of the earth. (Rev 6:7-8)

When the pale (ashen) horse was released for its mission, John clearly saw its rider's name – death (incidentally, this is the only rider that had a name). John further reported that Hades was following him. Given his description, it is unclear what John actually saw. Some Biblical background there may be needed to unravel what is written here.

The Hebrew behind the Greek Θάνατος (*thanatos*) translated as "death" and ᾅδης (*hades*) translated as "Hades" are Hebrew words מות (*mot*) and שאול (*sheol*). In Hosea 13:14, we read: "Shall I ransom them from the power of Sheol? Shall I redeem them from death? O Death, where are your thorns? O Sheol, where is your sting?" It is not unusual to fuse Death and Sheol together and speak of them in almost synonymous terms. *Mot* and *Sheol* are occasionally mentioned and personified together (Is.28:15, 18; Hab.2:5, Ps.18:5-6, 49:14, 116:3).

But what is Sheol (שאול, *sheol*) in the Hebrew Bible? Simply put, it is a place of darkness where all the dead go and wait until the time of final judgment and redemption. It is often translated simply as a "grave" When the Hebrew Scriptures were translated into Greek, the word Hades (ᾅδης, *hades*) the "underworld" in Greek was used by Jewish sages to translate Hebrew idea of Sheol (שאול, *sheol*). Therefore Hades (ᾅδης, *hades*) idea is closely connected with the idea of dying and death itself (Is. 28:15, 18; Ps. 18:5; 49:14; 116:3).

In Torah, when Jacob thinks that his beloved Joseph died, he exclaims, "I shall go down to Sheol (שאול, *sheol*) to my son" (Gen 37:35). But even between death and resurrection, the dead in Sheol are not without God's presence, "If I ascend to heaven, you are there; if I make my bed in Sheol, behold, you are there" (Psalm 139:8). Therefore, it is clear that Sheol (שאול) is a temporary realm, a holding place in which the dead await the day of judgment and resurrection. As explained before Sheol (*Hades*) and Hell *(Gehinmom)* should not be confused or fused together.

When Jesus describes "hell" in Mark 9:48 as a place "where the worm does not die, and the fire is not quenched," he quotes from Isaiah's vision. Isaiah 66:22-

24 describes future creation, "... new heavens and the new earth, which I make, will endure before me," declares the Lord... All mankind will come to bow down before me; they will go out and look at the corpses of the people who have rebelled against me. For their worm will not die and their fire will not be extinguished; and they will be an abhorrence (דראון; *deraon*) to all flesh" This "abhorrence" of the wicked is something that happens after judgment and after the resurrection of all who awaited that day in Sheol.

Daniel 12:2 also spoke of this moment, "And many of those who sleep in the dust of the ground will awake, these to everlasting life, but the others to disgrace and everlasting contempt (דראון; *deraon*)". This is the everlasting contempt that people refer to as "Hell" in English, which is different from Sheol in which all dead end up.

So, this death Θάνατος (*thanatos*) rider was given authority over a quarter of the earth to destroy life by 1) sword, 2) famine, 3) pestilence, and 4) wild beasts. This verse (vs.8) is highly significant to see the big picture since it strongly connects the text of Revelation with the words of Ezekiel. We must keep in mind that the anti-idolatry theme, which is prevalent in the early chapters of Revelation, will continue to resurface and will be developed throughout the rest of the book. Even here in chapters 6 and 7, that deal with the opening of the seven seals. Compromising with paganism is always a temptation. And Israel has struggled with this for many years. We read God's warnings to Jerusalem about succumbing to the idolatry of the nations around her in Ezekiel:

21 For thus says the Lord God, "How much
more when I send My four severe judgments
against Jerusalem: sword, famine, wild beasts
and plague to cut off man and beast from it! 22
Yet, behold, survivors will be left in it who will
be brought out, both sons and daughters.
Behold, they are going to come forth to you
and you will see their conduct and actions; then
you will be comforted for the calamity which I
have brought against Jerusalem for everything
which I have brought upon it. 23 Then they
will comfort you when you see their conduct
and actions, for you will know that I have not
done in vain whatever I did to it," declares the
Lord God. (Ezekiel 14:21-23)

We can clearly see that 'How much more when I send
My four severe judgments against Jerusalem: sword,
famine, wild beasts and plague to cut off man and beast
from it" is an almost verbatim quotation in Rev. 6:8b.
(Authority was given to them over a fourth of the
earth, to kill with sword and with famine and
with pestilence and by the wild beasts of the earth.) As
this four-fold judgment fell on the nation, it affected
both the faithful and the unfaithful among them.

Remember that idolatry was the main problem among
all of the seven assemblies mentioned in Revelation.
Therefore, the emphasis of the seven seals of judgment
is highly relevant and fits extremely well with the rest of
the book. While this part of Revelation is probably
based on Ezekiel, both books actually also draw from
the Torah, from Leviticus, where harsh national

disciplinary penalties for idolatry are explicitly stated (notice especially vs. 30). We read in Leviticus:

> 18 "If also after these things you do not obey Me, then I will punish you seven times more for your sins... 21 'If then, you act with hostility against Me and are unwilling to obey Me, I will increase the plague on you seven times according to your sins. 22 I will let loose among you the beasts of the field, which will bereave you of your children and destroy your cattle and reduce your number so that your roads lie deserted. 23 'And if by these things you are not turned to Me, but act with hostility against Me, 24 then I will act with hostility against you; and I, even I, will strike you seven times for your sins. 25 I will also bring upon you a sword which will execute vengeance for the covenant; and when you gather together into your cities, I will send pestilence among you, so that you shall be delivered into enemy hands... 'Yet if in spite of this you do not obey Me, but act with hostility against Me, 28 then I will act with wrathful hostility against you, and I, even I, will punish you seven times for your sins... 30 I then will destroy your high places, and cut down your incense altars, and heap your remains on the remains of your idols, for My soul shall abhor you." (Leviticus 26:18-26)

The sin of idolatry elicits harsh punishments because it undermines the very core of what is true. It warps the reality and robs God of the glory that is due to him.

When the Lamb broke the fifth seal, I saw underneath the altar the souls of those who had

been slain because of the word of God, and
because of the testimony which they had
maintained; and they cried out with a loud voice,
saying, "How long, O Lord, holy and true, will You
refrain from judging and avenging our blood
on those who dwell on the earth?" (Rev 6:9-10)

Not all seals had to do with a judgment that would fall on the righteous and unrighteous alike. The fourth seal was clearly meant as a judgment only against the wicked to avenge the blood and suffering of the righteous. John saw people under the altar of God waiting for justice – these are the people who were persecuted for their trust and absolute allegiance to the only living and true God. Their persecution and suffering is no doubt tied to their refusal to worship idols. What is not at all surprising is that they were demanding vengeance and justice from the holy and just God. We see a similar anticipation/demand for justice in Psalm 58. There are other imprecatory or "judgment-demanding" psalms such as 5, 10, 17, 35, 59, 69, 70, 79, 83, 109, 129, 137, 140).:

> O God, shatter their teeth in their mouth;
> Break out the fangs of the young lions, O Lord.
> 7 Let them flow away like water that runs off;
> When he aims his arrows, let them be as
> headless shafts. 8 Let them be as a snail
> which melts away as it goes along, Like the
> miscarriages of a woman which never see the
> sun… 10 The righteous will rejoice when he
> sees the vengeance; He will wash his feet in the
> blood of the wicked. 11 And men will say,
> 'Surely there is a reward for the righteous;

Surely there is a God who judges on earth!'"
(Psalm 58:6-11)

Notice how this psalm connects vengeance upon the
wicked with testimony for the bystanders of the world.
If the blood of the righteous is avenged, they will no
doubt say – there is a God who judges the earth, and
there is a reward for being righteous. It is important to
see the demand for punishment of the wicked does not
arise from a desire for personal revenge. Rather calls for
justice is to protect God's own reputation among the
people that witnessed the injustices. In 1 Enoch 22:5-8
we see what seems to be a common theme in Jewish
martyrological material – the divine avenging of the
blood of the righteous:

> "And I saw the spirits of the sons of men who
> were dead; and their voices reached to heaven,
> while they were accusing. Then I inquired of
> Raphael, an angel who was with me, and said,
> whose spirit is that the voice of which reaches
> to heaven, and accuses? He answered, saying,
> this is the spirit of Abel who was slain by Cain
> his brother; and who will accuse that brother,
> until his seed be destroyed from the face of the
> earth; Until his seed perish from the seed of
> the human race." (1 Enoch 22:5-8)

The same martyrological thought develops into the idea
of a collective voice, beseeching God for justice that is
very similar to what we encounter in the book of
Revelation. We continue to read in 1 Enoch 47:1-4:

> "And in those days shall have ascended the
> prayer of the righteous, and the blood of the
> righteous from the earth before the Lord of

Spirits. In those days the holy ones who dwell above in the heavens Shall unite with one voice and supplicate and pray and praise, and give thanks and bless the name of the Lord of Spirits On behalf of the blood of the righteous which has been shed, and that the prayer of the righteous may not be in vain before the Lord of Spirits, that judgment may be done unto them, and that they may not have to suffer forever. In those days I saw the Head of Days when He seated himself upon the throne of His glory, And the books of the living were opened before Him: and all His host which is in heaven above and His counselors stood before Him, and the hearts of the holy were filled with joy; because the number of the righteous had been offered, and the prayer of the righteous had been heard, and the blood of the righteous been required before the Lord of Spirits." (1 Enoch 47:1-4)

Whether in Revelation or in 1 Enoch, written three centuries earlier, the idea of martyrs, who stood up and maintained the oneness of God among the idols and lost their lives, is tied to the notion of God's character. This principle of justice has been in play since the days of Cain and Abel.

And there was given to each of them a white robe; and they were told that they should rest for a little while longer, until the number of their fellow servants and their brethren who were to be killed even as they had been, would be completed also. (Rev 6:11)

Just like the twenty-four elders ("...upon the thrones I saw twenty-four elders sitting, clothed in white garments" (Rev.4:4), so are those who have been martyred because of God's word and their testimony. They also have the right to wear white garments. In Revelation 7:9, we read that John beheld "a great multitude, which no one could count, from every nation and all tribe and peoples and tongues, standing before the throne and before the Lamb, clothed in white robes."

These righteous will continue crying out to God for justice. Later in Revelation 12:11, we read of the "saints" (קְדֹשִׁים, *kedoshim*) overcoming the evil one through "the blood of the Lamb and because of the word of their testimony, and they did not love their life even when faced with death." The reason for not avenging their blood right away is probably the same reason why God did not avenge the blood of his prophets long ago.

> 49 "For this reason also the wisdom of God said, 'I will send to them prophets and apostles, and some of them they will kill and some they will persecute, 50 so that the blood of all the prophets, shed since the foundation of the world, may be charged against this generation, 51 from the blood of Abel to the blood of Zechariah, who was killed between the altar and the house of God; yes, I tell you, it shall be charged against this generation.'" (Luke 11:49-51)

We see that collective punishment for the sins of many generations is sometimes poured out upon one generation chosen for such a punishment. While we may be tempted to see this as unfair, the ancients probably saw it in terms of God's long-suffering and withholding his anger, delaying justice on purpose Sins go unpunished because God's mercy and patience is great. But there is a limit to everything - certainly to God's patience, and judgment is necessary for God to be who he is.

One excellent example of such justice is given in Genesis 15:16, where God explains to Abraham why he cannot yet take possession of the Promised Land. This was because the "iniquity of the Amorites is not yet full." God's long-suffering should never be confused with his inability to render a fitting, in this case, a harsh, judgment. This is not a sign of weakness but strength. When Joshua finally brought the Israelites into the land 400 years later, God commanded him to wipe out everything, leaving nothing breathing, nothing alive. Seems extreme? Judgment took a very long time to come, hundreds and hundreds of years of second chances, but when it came, it was devastating.

Speaking in the name of "Isaiah" in the Ascension of Isaiah, the author reports that in the seventh heaven where the throne of God is, there is a storehouse of all righteous people from the time of Adam. In *Sepher ha-Razim* 7:1-3, we read this most interesting idea:

> "The seventh firmament, all of it is seven-fold light, and from its light all the seven heavens shine. Within it is the throne of glory, set on the four glorious Hayot (living beings). Also within it are the storehouse of lives, and the storehouse of souls." (Asc. Is. 9:7)

In a Jewish prayer for vengeance for murder, found on tombstones from Delos in Greece, dating to the 1 BCE, we read something that fits well with our text:

> "I call upon and pray the Most High God, the Lord of the spirits and of all flesh, against those who with guile murdered or poisoned the wretched, untimely lost Heraclea, shedding her innocent blood wickedly: that it may so with them that murdered or poisoned her, and with their children: O Lord that sees all things, and ye angels of God, Thou before whom every soul is afflicted this same day with supplication: That Thou may avenge the innocent blood and require it again right speedily!"[15]

Given the anti-pagan sentiment of the book of Revelation and its affiliation of Rome with Babylon, this parallel from Sibylline Oracles should also be considered:

> "For a heavenly eternal destruction will come upon you, O Babylon, One day, from above … you will be filled with blood, as you yourself formerly poured out the blood of good men and righteous men, whose blood even now cries out to high heaven." (Sib. Or. 3:307-313)

The idea of vengeance is prevalent in all near eastern societies. But for the Jews of the Second Temple era, this was not revenge; this was (צֶדֶק, *tzedek*) justice, equity, righteousness restored.

---

[15] Sylloge Inscriptionum Graecarum: 1181

I looked when He broke the sixth seal, and there was a great earthquake; and the sun became black as sackcloth made of hair, and the whole moon became like blood; and the stars of the sky fell to the earth, as a fig tree casts its unripe figs when shaken by a great wind. The sky was split apart like a scroll when it is rolled up, and every mountain and island were moved out of their places. (Rev 6:12-14)

The judgment brought about by this last horse and its rider amounts to a complete dissolution of the cosmos. This description uses normal vocabulary and concepts taken from Israel's prophets. There are many relevant background passages (Is. 13:10-13; 24:1-6; 19-23, 34:4; Ezek. 32:6-8; Joel 3:15-16, Hab.3:6-11) but consider these two examples:

> And all the host of heaven will wear away, and the sky will be rolled up like a scroll; all their hosts will also wither away as a leaf withers from the vine, or as one withers from the fig tree." (Isaiah 34:4) "The sun will be turned into darkness, and the moon into blood, before the great and awesome day of the LORD comes. (Joel 2:31)

In the Testament of Moses, we have another apocalyptic reading:

> "Then shall the Heavenly One arise from the seat of His kingdom, and come forth from His holy habitation, with wrath and indignation for His children's sake. And the earth shall tremble and quake to its utmost borders; and the lofty

mountains shall be humbled and shaken, and the valleys shall sink. The sun shall give no light, and shall turn into darkness; the horns of the moon shall be broken, and she shall be turned into blood, and the circle of the stars shall be confounded. The sea shall retreat to the abyss, the springs of water shall fail, and the rivers shall be dried up; because the Most High, the Eternal, the only God, shall arise and come manifestly to chastise the nations and to destroy their idols." (The Testament of Moses 159-160).

Here we have a remarkable similarity that casts aside all doubt concerning the lack of literary dependence. John, as the human author of the book of Revelation, interacted with Torah and the prophetic material both consciously and subconsciously. The things he saw he described in the way his mind had perceived, absorbed, and memorized the Holy Scriptures of ancient Israel. Whether or not this is meant to be literal or figurative is impossible to determine. The message of the prophecy and the vision is true; however, whether or not its actual fulfillment is literal is not clear.

Then the kings of the earth and the great men and the commanders and the rich and the strong and every slave and free man hid themselves in the caves and among the rocks of the mountains; and they said to the mountains and to the rocks, "Fall on us and hide us from the presence of Him who sits on the throne, and from the wrath of the Lamb; for the great day of their wrath has come, and who is able to stand?" (Rev 8:15-17)

People sometimes erroneously say that the God of the Hebrew Bible and the God of the New Testament are very different since the New Testament portrays God as far more gracious, merciful, and long-suffering, while the "Old Testament," the emphasis is on judgment, retribution, and law. Nothing can be farther from the truth. Such sentiment is completely inaccurate on many levels. The entire book of Revelation is a case in point when it comes to the New Testament writings. In this section, we see a scene of the ultimate judgment, the cosmic collapse and disintegration of all things as part of the disciplinary action of both God and the Lamb.

Fleeing from the presence of the one who sits on the throne and the Lamb, whose wrath has been fully and rightfully kindled, is present only here and in Rev. 20. This will indeed be a dreadful day when not only the poor, who generally are in need of protection and help, but also the mighty of this world find themselves in a situation where they need to run and hide, and they cannot find proper refuge. Their request is issued to the mountains to cover them with falling rocks. This is a terrible thing to request, but their suffering and fear pale in comparison to the dread they now feel before the LORD and the Lamb.

Lastly, the mighty of this world, fearing the wrath of the Lamb, evokes the imagery seen early in Revelation 5, where John was stopped from weeping by one of the elders who spoke to him: "Stop weeping; behold, the Lion that is from the tribe of Judah, the Root of David, has overcome so as to open the book and its seven seals." When he looked, he expected to see the Lion, but instead, he saw the Lamb.

In C.S. Lewis's famous "The Lion, The Witch and the Wardrobe," Susan asks Mr. Beaver about Aslan, the figure clearly representing Christ:

"Aslan is a lion - the Lion, the great Lion," said Mr. Beaver. "Oh," said Susan. "I'd thought he was a man. Is he - quite safe? I shall feel rather nervous about meeting a lion." "Safe?" said Mr. Beaver. "Who said anything about safe? 'Course he isn't safe. But he's good. He's the King, I tell you."

In Closing

We sincerely hope that this was a fruitful journey for you and that we were able to show not merely insights we see in this book but also teach a method of reading Revelation differently. We encourage everyone to read and re-read Revelation in its historic cultural setting, read it as a Jewish book, as a message to real people who were oppressed and persecuted. And we know that re-reading it in this light will produce fresh insights each time. That is what we encourage our readers to do as we now purposefully set such a trajectory.

MY REQUEST

Dear reader, may I ask you for a favor? Would you take three minutes of your time and provide encouraging feedback to other people about this book (assuming you like it so far, of course!)?

Here is how: Go to Amazon.com, find this book "Hebrew Insights from Revelation," and write a brief customer review!

After writing a review, please drop me a personal note and let me know - dr.eli.israel@gmail.com.

In His Grace,

Dr. Eli Lizorkin-Eyzenberg

Bibliography

Aune, David Edward. *Revelation 1-5, Volume 52A*. (United States: Zondervan), 2014.

Bauckham Richard, *The Climax of Prophecy*, (Bloomsbury Publishing Edinburgh), 1993.

Beale, G. K. *The Book of Revelation*. (United Kingdom: Eerdmans Publishing Company), 1999.

Beard, Mary et al., *Religions of Rome: Volume 2, A Sourcebook* (Cambridge University Press) 1998.

Charlesworth, James H. *The Old Testament Pseudepigrapha*. (United Kingdom: Hendrickson Publishers Marketing), 2010.

Collins, John J. *Between Athens and Jerusalem: Jewish Identity in the Hellenistic Diaspora* (Wm. B. Eerdmans Publishing, 2000).

Evans, Craig A, Stanley E. Porter, *Dictionary of New Testament Background*. (United Kingdom: IVP), 2020.

Goodman, Martin, Jeremy Cohen, and David Sorkin, *The Oxford Handbook of Jewish Studies* (Oxford University Press, Oxford) 2002.

Greenspoon, Leonard Jay, Ronald Simkins, and Gerald Shapiro, *Food and Judaism* (Creighton University Press) 2005.

Harland, Philip A. *Associations, Synagogues, and Congregations: Claiming a Place in Ancient Mediterranean Society* (Fortress Press, 2003).

Jellinek, A. *Beth ha-midraš*, (United Kingdom), 1855.

Keener, Craig S. *Revelation.*(United States: Zondervan), 2000.

Koester, Craig R. *Revelation: A New Translation with Introduction and Commentary*. (United Kingdom: Yale University Press), 2014.

Levine. Amy-Jill and Marc Zvi Brettler, *The Jewish Annotated New Testament* (Oxford University Press), 2017.

Nickelsburg, George W. E. *Jewish Literature Between the Bible and the Mishnah: A Historical and Literary Introduction* (Fortress Press, 1981).

Osborne, Grant R. *Revelation: Baker Exegetical Commentary on the New Testament.* (United States: Baker Publishing Group), 2002.

Pate, C. Marvin. *Four Views on the Book of Revelation.* (United States: Zondervan Publishing House), 1998.

Tabor, James D. *How Christian is the New Testament Book of Revelation*, article in "Huffington Post", 2013.

Thompson, Leonard L. *Abingdon New Testament Commentaries: Revelation.* (United States: Abingdon Press), 2011.

Vanderkam, James C. *An Introduction to Early Judaism* (Wm. B. Eerdmans Publishing), 2001.

Printed in Great Britain
by Amazon

70479901R00108